1-2-3 SMOOTHIES

by Rita Bingham

Introduction by Tom Dickson of K-TEC, manufacturer of the best commercial smoothie equipment on the market!

1-2-3 Smoothies introduces easy smoothie recipes using wholesome *Fruits, Fruit Juice Concentrates, Grains,* and *Veggies*, which are very low in fat (usually only 2-3%) and cholesterol-FREE.

With these recipes, you can make nutritious drinks from NATURAL foods you're guaranteed to LOVE!

NATURAL MEALS PUBLISHING
Edmond, Oklahoma

ISBN 1-882314-14-X
$14.95

Library of Congress Catalog Card Number: 98-091515

Published by Natural Meals Publishing
Website: www. naturalmeals.com
E-mail: info@naturalmeals.com
OR sales@naturalmeals.com
Fax: 405.359.3492
Order Line: 888.232.6706

Printed in United States of America

Cover photo by Bozarth Photography

Illustrations by Clair Bingham

For:

My children who grew up drinking smoothies for breakfast and after school snacks (or whenever the urge struck!);

My grandchildren who live far away from me (so *their* moms can sneak nutritious ingredients into smoothies!).

Special Thanks to:

My husband and best friend, Clair for his great artwork, his wise counsel and his invaluable taste-testing;

Our daughters Ginni and Kimm, for their help in research, recipe development, giving their honest opinion, and typesetting;

My good friends Jayne Benkendorf and Devri Conlin for their careful proofreading and suggestions.

An Introduction

For over 10 years, K-TEC has been dedicated to producing home and commercial milling, mixing and blending equipment to make cooking easier.

The Smoothie Revolution of the 90's has been an exciting one for us, as our high-speed blenders are now creating smoothies in thousands of companies, including restaurants, coffee shops, and smoothie stores. These fruity concoctions are taking the country by storm. Why? Because they are light, refreshing, and filling, and a great way to get "5 a day" of the essential fruits and veggies recommended by the U.S. government.

It's no secret that we need to eat more nutritious foods if we want our health to improve. Rita's books *Natural* **Meals In Minutes** and **Country Beans** are filled with all-natural recipes using whole grains, beans, fresh fruits and vegetables—the low-fat, high-fiber foods we're hearing so much about these days as doctors and scientists recognize their healing and strengthening effects. In "1-2-3- Smoothies," Rita follows her tradition of providing us with nutritious recipes. These drinks are not the run-of-the-mill kind that supply little more than excess empty calories — these are good FOR you as well as GOOD! Healthy add-ins are a perfect way to make sure you get a full day's supply of important nutrients.

The RX smoothies section in this book is full of delicious drinks to supply healing nutrients to kids and reluctant adults. What great medicine for "what ails 'em!"

Nut, seed, bean and grain "milks" are easier to digest and less likely than cow's milk to cause or irritate food allergies and sensitivities. These can be purchased from a health food store, or made fresh at home in only minutes using our Kitchen Mill and Champ blender.

Each smoothie in this book is a sweet treat by itself, perfect for a snack, a dessert, or a whole meal. For special occasions, you can add ice cream or flavored yogurt to make any recipe into a dessert smoothie (just make sure your "special occasion" isn't every day!). These frosty drinks are sure to please both young and old.

Tom Dickson
K-TEC, Lindon, UT

About the Author

Since 1966, Rita Bingham has taught and encouraged healthy eating. She carries on the tradition of her mother, Esther Dickey, who over 30 years ago wrote **Passport to Survival** (a comprehensive guide to using and storing basic foods), and Skills for Survival (a self-sufficiency manual of basic skills for surviving major and minor disasters).

Continuing in the tradition of her nutrition-oriented family, Rita uses wholesome, basic foods and imaginative techniques to create fast, high fiber recipes for every meal of the day, even snacks and desserts! Her husband and 5 children, as well as thousands of seminar participants, have given Rita's recipes rave reviews.

Rita has written and self-published three cookbooks on healthful eating; produced a training video to demonstrate some of the many ways nutritious foods can be prepared in a minimum amount of time; written articles for newspapers and magazines; co-hosted a radio show providing information and recipes for healthy eating. She has consulted for companies to help solve their food problems and create marketable products. Rita has also provided training on how to include nutritious foods in weight loss programs.

Many seminar participants and customers ask if Rita and her family REALLY eat the healthy meals found in her books or if she just enjoys making up recipes and writing books. The answer is YES...the family enjoys this type of food (most of the time). They've all strayed at times from the high-fiber "back to basics" foods to eating "normal" foods (the white, the sugary and the fatty ones), but they all admit that good food makes them FEEL good and greatly improves health (making a visit to the doctor a *very* rare occasion), as well as keeping weight normal. When the children were small, they loved to learn about the nutrients in foods. One particularly patient neighbor learned to hide his smile and put on his serious face when the children regularly came to tell him the health benefits of foods like whole wheat, sweet potatoes, alfalfa sprouts, or brown rice. ...and YES! Rita does enjoy making up recipes and writing books. Finding ways to make more nutritious meals in less time has been a lifelong hobby for Rita, and she enjoys the challenge of sneaking healthy foods into traditional recipes.

More and more people are becoming more aware of how good foods help them feel better physically, mentally and emotionally. The *Natural Meals In Minutes* style of eating is designed for those who recognize the importance of taking responsibility for their health and well being. Does this way of eating take more time than opening a can or a box? Certainly, but your health is worth it! ❤

Table of Contents

HOW TO READ THE NUTRITIONAL INFORMATION
Cal. 150 Fat .7g Carb. 30g Pro. 6g Pot. 170mg Vit. C 875mg Fib. 3.3g

Cal. - the number of calories in one serving. Even though packaged foods use a 2,000 calories per day figure as the "norm" for women, that amount is actually for growing children and very active adults. Most women do very well on 1,300 to 1,500 calories per day when eating wholesome foods.

Fat - the grams of fat per serving. Although the USRDA for fat is 65 grams, research shows this figure to be too high for the sedentary "American" lifestyle. Most people maintain proper weight or lose excess pounds when they consume only 25-30 grams of fat per day. Active people burn more fat so they can get away with consuming more fat without gaining weight. According to Dr. Dean Ornish and thousands of other physicians, a less than 10% fat diet is ideal for regaining health and losing excess weight. The body actually needs few, if any, added fats, as whole foods contain adequate amounts of fat for proper growth and nourishment.

Carb. - the grams of carbohydrate available in one serving to supply the body with energy. They are found almost exclusively in plant foods. Higher amounts are good if you're eating whole foods (NOT foods made with refined white flour or white sugar) for quick energy that won't cause a quick high, followed by a rock bottom low. On a 2000 calorie diet, about 1200 calories should come from carbohydrates.

Pro. - the number of grams of protein in one serving. If you worry about adequate protein intake on a vegetarian diet, research has shown that it is impossible NOT to get enough protein when you use wholesome beans and grains on a daily basis. (The USDA figure of 65 grams of protein has been proven to be higher than necessary for proper growth and development. Excess protein puts extra stress on the kidneys and liver. Recent studies have shown 35 grams to be adequate, since the body makes its OWN protein from amino acids found in all foods.)

Pot. - the milligrams of potassium in one serving. This mineral is important for a healthy nervous system, maintaining stable blood pressure and in the transmission of electro-chemical impulses. It helps with dry skin, muscle fatigue and weakness, water retention, and high cholesterol.

Vit. C - the milligrams of vitamin C in one serving. This essential vitamin is an antioxidant that attacks free radicals, protects against infection, enhances immunity, helps prevent cancer and other diseases, and promotes the healing of wounds.

Fib. - the grams of fiber in one serving. Most fruit is not high in fiber, but an average of 25 grams of fiber per day is *essential*. Eat *whole* foods — whole wheat, brown rice and other grains, beans, unpeeled fruit and vegetables, and at least 1/4 of your food raw. ❤

FORWARD

Who loves smoothies? As my children say, "Nobody doesn't love Smoothies!" **Nutrition** used to mean "boring." **Natural** used to mean "tasteless." "**Fast**" food used to be a bad four-letter word. Not any more!

It doesn't matter whether you're young and trying to keep up with kids and a job, or no longer young and concerned about cardiovascular health; a body builder or an aerobics buff; a little kid, teenager, or a big kid; health-conscious or weight conscious! If you love great taste, you'll LOVE these creamy, energizing smoothies! **1-2-3 Smoothies** blend fun with food the whole family will enjoy. They're Super Nutritious, Super Filling, and Super Quick...for SUPER Health!

DON'T SKIP BREAKFAST—SIP A SMOOTHIE!

Too many people these days skip breakfast - the meal that should supply energy and brain power for the best half of the day! **1-2-3 Smoothies** are smooooooth fruit drinks blended from fresh or frozen fruits and fruit juice concentrates. They are very satisfying, and with the addition of Juice Plus+ (a complete blend of active enzymes, vitamins and minerals) and protein in the form of tofu, protein powders or nuts and seeds, you'll have a nutrient-dense (that meals filling!) meal or snack.

1-2-3 SMOOTHIES - THE PERFECT FOOD?

Is there one perfect breakfast-- perfect afternoon snack-- perfect meal-on-the-run--perfect way to sneak nutritious vitamins and other important nutrients into a finicky eater? YES! It's a **1-2-3 Smoothie**! Chock full of nutritious energy-boosting wholesome ingredients, these delicious, nutritious drinks are the hottest COOL healthy treats ever! (Check out the nutritional data included with each recipe.) Each one is a fresh blend of fruity fun. What's more, they're made with 100% natural ingredients - no preservatives, no sugar or artificial sweeteners, and no added fat.

DO-IT-YOURSELF ENTERTAINMENT

1-2-3 Smoothies are so easy to make, even young children can blend their own all-natural treats. What's not to love? Kids start with frozen chunks of fresh fruit, add delicious juices, punch the right buttons and presto! they've made their own frosty concoction that's actually GOOD for them!

By the time they've made two or three, they'll want to start experimenting, so supply them with a few options and let them turn a smoothie into a science project as they fiddle with adding a little of this and a little of that, substituting one fruit or juice for another; a little ice for none at all; nuts or no nuts; water, milk or our special "milks" made from grains or soybeans. Improvising is an important skill and making up original smoothies is a good way for kids of all ages to start learning that recipes are made to be changed! ❤

SERVING SIZES

One serving of each delicious, nutritious smoothie is 12 ounces. Most smoothies supply 2 servings of fruit (or juice) and an average of 200 calories.

One serving of fruit, according to the U.S.RDA guidelines, is equal to 1 apple, 1 orange, 1 banana, (the equivalent of about 1 cup of chopped fruit), one 8 ounce glass of juice, or 2 ounces of frozen 100% fruit juice concentrate. Each person should have a **minimum** of 2 fresh (uncooked and unsweetened) fruits per day. Remember to add lots of fresh veggies too—especially the green, leafy ones.

Research shows **at least** four servings of fruit and five servings of vegetables (mostly raw) are necessary to rebuild the immune system and protect the body from cancer and other degenerative diseases. These foods are responsible for providing most of the vitamins and minerals necessary for proper growth and good health. ❤

1-2-3 SMOOTHIES
A STEP TOWARD WELLNESS

 I have friends who say they enjoy good health, yet they take prescription and over-the-counter drugs on a daily basis. If a visit to a doctor or a hospital eliminates symptoms so they can continue to work, or keep their children in school, then they feel they are "well." Wellness is far more than not being "sick." Pills and potions (whether from "natural" sources or in the form of drugs) have their place, but they are most often used to treat symptoms, while the *reason* for the symptoms is ignored.

Health is undeniably linked to the foods we eat. Our daily food choices can improve our health or destroy it. Most of us eat what tastes or looks good without giving thought to whether it IS good (for us). Cheryl

> Health (good or bad) is undeniably linked to the foods we eat. Our daily food choices can improve our health or destroy it.

Townsley, author of **Food Smart!**, cites research showing that 80 percent of all deaths are in some way diet-related. (This means that the things we eat — or don't eat — cause diseases that eventually cause 80 percent of all deaths!) A strong body is able to mend itself. How do we gain a strong body? By becoming educated so we can make smart food choices. This is *critical* to improving health. The fact that you're reading this section is proof that you are interested in making better food choices. The recipes in this book will help you get on the road to better health. When you're ready to try eating more wholesome meals, the recipes in my other books, **Country Beans** and *Natural* **Meals In Minutes**, will supply you with hundreds of good food choices for every meal of the day, including snacks and desserts.

Mrs. Townsley gives 17 steps to help get you started in the process of making smart food choices. The following is a summary:

One — Tour a Health Food Store, Find a Buying Club, or a Food Co-op
Health food includes fresh produce (organic when possible), whole grains and beans, and packaged foods made without additives and chemicals. (I am amazed at how much *better* foods taste that have been grown organically!) Companies that sell mills and equipment often have sources for whole grains, beans, seeds and nuts. Buying in bulk saves BIG over health food store prices. See the Equipment and Suppliers section at the end of this book for some good sources.

Two — Keep a Food Diary
When you are just starting out, it's a good idea to keep a record of the foods eaten (and any reactions noted). This helps get an accurate picture of how much of what kind of food you are actually eating.

Three — Read Labels
Besides checking out the fat content, take a look at the chemicals, preservatives and additives in the foods you eat on a daily basis. Do you *need* preserving? (Probably not, unless you've already achieved perfection!) A simple rule of thumb is to buy products made from FOOD, not chemicals.

Four — Eat More Vegetables
The more processed foods you eat, the more you crave. Vegetables (especially dark-colored ones) contain minerals essential to good health. Vegetable smoothies are a good way to clean off your taste buds and start enjoying "real" food. Follow up with a fresh green salad (use leaf lettuce, not iceberg). Eat most of your veggies raw.

> The more processed foods you eat, the more you crave. Vegetables (especially dark-colored ones) contain minerals essential to good health.

Five — Eat More Fruits
Fruits are a good source of vitamins. Buy them ripe (or pick them ripe if you happen to be so lucky to live where fruits grow) and eat them raw, and peel only those with inedible peelings, such as bananas, pineapple, mango, cantaloupe, etc.

Six — Eat Food That Has Been Cleaned

When you buy produce from the store, do you know who's hands have touched it and where those hands have been? Clean produce is essential. I use 20 drops of Nutribiotic GSE, grapefruit seed extract in a quart of water and spray on all produce to kill any bacteria and wash away any chemicals, fertilizers and pesticides on the outside. After a thorough washing, food is ready to eat. (One 2-oz. bottle costs only $10.95, plus $3.50 s&h, and can also be used to purify up to 126 gallons of water! Call 1-888-232-6706 for more information.)

Seven — Store Foods Correctly to Prevent Spoilage

Years ago a doctor advised me to "eat foods capable of rotting and eat them before they do." Live, healthy foods need to be eaten as soon as they are ripe (or refrigerated). Nuts, fresh herbs and freshly ground flours should be refrigerated or frozen.

Eight — Eat Food in the Healthiest Form Possible

The closer food is to its raw form, the more nutritious it is. Only raw foods contain enzymes which are essential for digestion and healing.

Nine — Drink Fresh Juices as Much as Possible

Fresh fruits and veggies make the very best juices. Juices and smoothies are an easy way to increase raw food intake and provide a rich supply of vitamins and minerals. Bottoms up on those smoothies!

Ten — Reduce Your Intake of Sugar!

Sugar makes ME crazy! I don't like being a fruitcake, and if I have one bite of a sugary something, I want ten more, so I have to stay completely away from sugar except on rare occasions. Honey is a great substitute, because it doesn't result in addictions like sugar does, but it's not good to

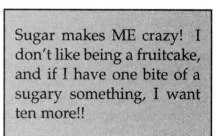

Sugar makes ME crazy! I don't like being a fruitcake, and if I have one bite of a sugary something, I want ten more!!

have too much of any sweetener. Honey is not recommended for children under 1 year. (See **Food Smart!** for a list of other acceptable sweeteners.)

Eleven — Reduce Fats and Use Good Oils
Eliminate hydrogenated fats completely. They actually *increase* cholesterol. These fats are in virtually all margarines, shortening and most processed foods. Don't fry foods in oil. Use water or vegetable broth. Use a 2 to 1 mixture of lecithin and canola oil for oiling pans.

Twelve — Eat Whole Grain Pastas and Breads
Pasta and breads made from white flour turn into glue in the intestinal tract because they have had the fiber and essential nutrients milled out of them. Buy **whole grain** products or make your own. (Many labels say "whole wheat bread" but list

> Pasta and breads made from white flour turn into glue in the intestinal tract because they have had the fiber and essential nutrients milled out of them.

"enriched flour" as one of the ingredients, meaning they've only added **some** whole wheat flour.)

Thirteen — Eat More Whole Grains, Legumes, Seeds and Sprouts
To avoid food allergies and to add variety and extra nutrients, try some different **grains** like millet, whole oats, rye, barley. Most can be used interchangeably when making quick breads. Legumes can be sprouted and eaten raw, or cooked.

Most people think they don't have time to cook **beans**, but my book, **Country Beans**, introduces bean, pea and lentil flours that cook in only 3 minutes. These flours are excellent for cream soups, sauces, dips and gravies.

Seeds and Nuts make great snacks. Pumpkin, sunflower and pine nut are our favorites. Raw is best, but if you must have them toasted, toast half and mix with the raw. **Sprouts** are easy to grow and in many places can be purchased in grocery stores. My favorite sprouts are mung bean, clover and buckwheat. For sprouting instructions, see *Natural* **Meals In Minutes**, p. 82. Sprouts are the freshest live food you can eat and an excellent source of chlorophyll as well as enzymes to aid in digestion.

Fourteen — Reduce Your Intake of Meat

The chemicals and steroids found in commercial meats are more harmful than the fat the meats contain. If you can't find a source for meats without chemicals, steroids and growth hormones, then think twice or maybe ten times before eating it. Many people manage well without any meat.

Fifteen — Eat Less Dairy

Dairy products are hard for the human body to digest. The calcium in milk is virtually inaccessible because the enzymes have been destroyed in the pasteurization process. If you can't buy certified raw milk, then eliminate it or use it very sparingly. People who have quit using dairy products have experienced fewer coughs and colds and decreased allergy symptoms. In our family, the champion snorer has stopped snoring!

In this book, you'll find recipes to make your own alternative milks. Or, they can be purchased at a health food store.

Sixteen — Increase Your Water Consumption

To determine how much water you should be drinking, divide your weight by 2 to get the number of ounces. Divide by 8 to get the number of cups to drink every day.

Very few people actually drink the recommended 8 glasses of water per day. Most of those who do are drinking "city" water which is full of harmful chemicals. Drink only pure water. Drink most of your water at other than mealtime to give foods a chance to digest properly. Water dilutes the digestive enzymes, allowing foods to pass through the body too quickly without being broken down and utilized.

Seventeen — No-No Foods to Avoid

Keep a food diary and see how many foods from the following list you consume. Take one step at a time. (If you're adding IN whole foods, it will be easier to eliminate refined ones.)

Caffeine

Alcohol

Foods containing preservatives, additives and chemicals

High-sodium products

MSG (monosodium glutamate)

Food coloring

Refined sugar, and all products using it

White flour and all products using it

Margarine, shortening and high-fat products

Solvent derived oils (all expeller pressed oils will state that fact on the label)

White rice

Carbonated beverages

Salt-cured or smoked foods (foods containing nitrates and nitrites

Some of the above material was taken from **Food Smart** and reprinted by permission. ❤

Rita's 5-A-Day For WELLNESS

1. HEALTHY EATING

Eat the best foods available—whole grains, beans, seeds, and 5-9 servings of a variety of vegetables and fruits—with as many "live" (raw) foods as possible; eliminate altered fats and refined foods; replace individual vitamin/mineral supplements with Juice Plus+, a powdered juice product containing active enzymes and fiber; regulate calorie intake to energy output.

Note: DNA (the blueprint used in cell duplication) damage is caused by free radicals produced by the body in response to stress, overprocessed foods, polluted water and air. In a recent study at Brigham Young University, Juice Plus+ significantly reduced DNA damage (by 66%), even in people who smoked. Another study showed that supplementation with Juice Plus+ significantly improves major immune functions.

2. EXERCISE

Walk briskly 20-30 minutes a day, 3-5 days a week, and stretch any and all tense, tight muscles (check out yoga and biofeedback!).

3. POSITIVE THINKING

Replace "can't," "shouldn't," "ought to," or "afraid to" with positives. Our minds are marvelous at obeying our commands, but most of our commands are negative. If we tell ourselves how fat, how sick, and how depressed we are, our minds will obey and we WILL be. If we tell ourselves how healthy and strong we are, that we are able to think quickly and clearly, that our immune system is growing stronger each day, etc., those positive things will come to pass!

4. LOWER STRESS

We all need stress, but when daily stress wears us down rather than invigorates us, it becomes negative stress. Breathing becomes shallow, upsetting the body's oxygen balance. The immune system breaks down. Muscles become tense and tight, thereby restricting the flow of blood and causing soreness and additional tension...a vicious cycle that sets in motion a chain of events leading to illness. Ask yourself "Is there some stress I can learn to avoid or eliminate?"

5. RIGHTEOUS LIVING

Everyone needs the support of believing in a higher being who created us, loves us, knows our needs and answers our prayers. We all have a need to be loved and we never feel more loved than when we give love away through service and genuinely caring for others. We are being watched over and protected. The challenges we are given are meant to strengthen us. We can and will feel at peace when we learn to accept what we are given and make the best of it. ❤

SMOOTHIES 'N' KIDS — DO THEY MIX?

Kids LOVE smoothies and most kids love creating and blending their own concoctions. My children were much more willing to drink something nutritious once they had studied about the value of an ingredient.

Use smoothies as a learning experience—learn **English** (how to read a recipe); **math** (how to measure, fractions, multiplication, division); **physics** (what happens when you add too much of something and the drink flows over the top!; and how flavors blend or react with others); **science** (what happens when frozen fruits and ice are added to liquids; how textures differ depending on how long the mixture is blended); **nutrition** (what nutrients the ingredients contain and what they're used for by the body); and **health** (what vitamins and minerals the body needs and the physical effects noticed when the body is properly nourished).

How old should children be to make smoothies on their own? Very young children can assist an older child or grownup in adding ingredients and pushing buttons. As soon as a child can demonstrate an ability to push the right buttons and remember to put the lid on *before* pushing buttons, give him/her the opportunity. What a thrill it is to watch a young child make a delightful creation. How exciting for a child to start revising recipes—substituting a peach for a banana, strawberries for blackberries, etc.

Kids especially need the add-ins suggested in these recipes. Help them research what would be best for them and why, then let them choose their own based on their needs. Let them experiment to find out just how much nutrition they can add and still LOVE their smoothies. ❤

GETTING STARTED

The Basic Ingredients

In this book, you'll find only 100% natural ingredients - no preservatives, no sugar or artificial sweeteners, and no added fats. These recipes call for fresh or frozen chunks of unsweetened fruit, 100% fruit juices, and "milk" made from soy, nuts, seeds, or grains. For an energy boost and to sneak in a little extra nutrition, some recipes call for added protein in the form of tofu, protein powders or nuts and seeds.

"Milks" used in these recipes

Many people are sensitive to or allergic to cow's milk (my family included), and we have often felt cheated because our favorite smoothie recipes didn't taste the same when we used water instead of milk. We started experimenting with making our own soy, nut and grain milks and found them to be great substitutes! (If you don't want to make your own, most health stores and some grocery stores now carry these milk substitutes.) We've included our favorites in the Milks section.

All milks are interchangeable in these recipes. If you normally use dairy products, you can use them in any of the recipes. If you'd rather not use tofu (or are allergic to soy products), you can add yogurt. If you're allergic to both, simply omit them.

Ice Cubes

When the recipe calls for an "ice cube," how big is it? When I first started making smoothies, I used ice from my ice cube trays. Now, most people have icemakers and the cubes are smaller, so I've included the information below so you can use either. In all recipes, ice cubes called for are ice maker cubes.

Two long, skinny ice cubes from my ice maker = 1 1/2 T. water or approximately 1 large, square ice cube from a tray. If in doubt, add less than you think you should, because it's easier to add more ice than to add more flavoring. ❤

ADD-INS

Since nutrients in pill and capsule form often pass through the body unused, nutrients in liquid, powder or oil form are much better for the body and can easily be added to a smoothie. However, many of them are *nasty!*

Most of the "supernutrients" are dark green in color (that's why we should be having at least one serving of dark green veggies every day) and while dark green on a plate may be appealing, a generous serving of spirulina turns a pleasing sunshine-yellow drink into brown mud. Adding a full day's supply of calcium powder (about 1 1/4 teaspoons per serving!) will make you want to chalk the sidewalk with your smoothie rather than drink it.

Some companies advertise 30 different products to be "added in" to smoothies for better health and nutrition. However, the 1/4 t. of lecithin and bee pollen that was added to my 24-oz. serving size smoothie didn't add enough extra nutrition to even count! If you

> Adding a full day's supply of calcium powder will make you want to chalk the sidewalk with your smoothie rather than drink it.

added enough of most of the "healthy" add-ins to really be healthy, the drinks wouldn't be very popular. It's still a good idea to add as many nutritious things as possible, but start with small quantities so you don't ruin a great smoothie.

I prefer to add ingredients like flaxseed oil, Juice Plus+, a powdered juice product containing active enzymes and fiber, vitamin C powder, acidophilus powder, brewer's yeast, and rice or soy protein powders (in moderation), because they are easy to hide. The nasty or grainy or greeney supplements I use in small amounts, or take some other way, thank you, so I can thoroughly enjoy my smoothies. If a smoothie has to taste like medicine, would you look forward to **your** daily dose????

RECOMMENDED
1-2-3 SMOOTHIE ADD-INS

ACIDOPHILUS POWDER
This is the "friendly" intestinal bacteria which aids in the digestion of food. It also helps reduce blood cholesterol levels, aids in the control and prevention of candidiasis (excess yeast in the body) and makes it easier for the body to absorb nutrients. The brand I use contains 2 billion live organisms per 1/4 teaspoon.

ALMONDS, CASHEWS, FILBERTS,
SUNFLOWER SEEDS, SESAME SEEDS
Most whole, raw nuts and seeds supply protein, "good" fat and fatty acids, calcium, iron, potassium and trace minerals. Soaked and/or sprouted nuts are easier to digest than dry nuts because enzymes have been activated and they are easier to chew properly. For a special treat, toast nuts or seeds and add to your smoothie a few during the last few seconds of

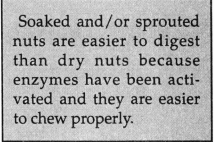

Soaked and/or sprouted nuts are easier to digest than dry nuts because enzymes have been activated and they are easier to chew properly.

blending. You'll get crunchy pieces to chew on that give a pleasant burst of nutty flavor.

ALOE VERA JUICE
We have used this for years to heal surface wounds such as cuts, eczema, poison ivy, burns, and stings, but it has also been helpful in stomach and intestinal problems as well as colon disorders. George's Always Active Aloe is a brand we like because it is tasteless. It can be added to any smoothie that calls for water, or use it in place of milk.

BREWER'S YEAST

This energy booster helps in metabolizing sugar, and has been shown to help in eczema, nervousness and fatigue. Rich in phosphorus, B vitamins, 16 amino acids, and a more than 13 different minerals. With over 50% protein content, this valuable product is a welcome nutrient in any smoothie. It has a mellow, nutty taste and goes well with nut milks.

> Brewer's Yeast is an energy booster that helps in metabolizing sugar, and has been shown to help in eczema, nervousness and fatigue.

CALCIUM POWDER

Calcium from milk and dairy products forces much of the phosphorus from the body, rendering the calcium unusable. Since the body needs calcium to function, the body takes it from the bones and joints, which leads to osteoporosis. Most people get enough calcium, but lack the trace minerals (found in leafy greens, spirulina, sprouts, wheat grass, barley grass, etc.) to utilize it properly. Adding a **little** calcium is OK in a smoothie, but don't try to add a full day's supply. The brand of calcium I use contains 450 mg. calcium and 250 mg. magnesium per 1/2 teaspoon. Calcium can be purchased as a liquid or a powder, plain or with magnesium. Remember, the body best utilizes calcium from fresh foods, especially figs, raisins, and all green, leafy vegetables.

DATES

Dates are excellent sweeteners for cakes, cookies and smoothies. Like most fruits, they are high in potassium and a good source of calories.

ESSENTIAL FATTY ACIDS (EFAs)

Heat destroys these essential building blocks necessary for health and that cannot be manufactured by the body. Every living cell needs essential fatty acids to rebuild and produce new cells. If you don't consume fatty meats, butter, baked goods with added oils, etc., adding EFAs to smoothies in the form of flaxseed oil, sesame seeds and nuts is the perfect way to insure that adequate quantities are consumed.

Sources: Nuts, seeds, legumes, sesame and soy oils, flaxseed and flaxseed oil, canola oil. Heating in any way, either in processing or in cooking, damages the fatty acids.

FLAXSEED OIL

The flaxseed is rich in omega-3 essential fatty acids, magnesium, potassium and fiber and a good source of zinc, B vitamins and protein. It has a pleasant, nutty taste that makes the whole or ground seeds an excellent addition to cooked or cold cereals, pancakes, muffins, salads, etc. The oil, when cold-pressed, is rich in fatty acids that have been known to lower cholesterol and triglyceride levels. Purchase the oil from a health food store and keep frozen or refrigerated.

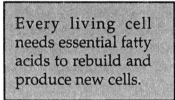

Every living cell needs essential fatty acids to rebuild and produce new cells.

Barlean's is my favorite brand. A surprising amount can be added to most drinks without any off-flavor. **Note:** While on vacation recently, I bought Barlean's flaxseed oil and it tasted like cod liver oil! If it doesn't smell nutty and *pleasant*, it isn't fresh.

LECITHIN

This nutrient is a lipid that is utilized by every cell of the body. It is especially valuable for older people and for those with high cholesterol and triglycerides. It comes in capsule form and in large or small granules. It is often used in breads and other processed foods. It allows harmful fats to be flushed from the body, protecting the heart and arteries from cholesterol buildup. It has been known to help improve brain function. Most lecithin comes from soybeans. It is also present in brewer's yeast, grains, and legumes.

OAT BRAN

Bran is the outside coat of the oat kernel, so it contains most of the fiber and nutrients. It helps lower cholesterol and adds a creamy texture to any smoothie. Adding oat bran to a smoothie gives it a "chunky" texture and is excellent when added with toasted sunflower seeds.

PROTEIN POWDERS

There are many vegetable-based protein powders on the market. Most are made from soy. While some are labeled as good for weight reduction, most are labeled as "food supplements" only, meaning that they are designed to supplement a diet of regular foods....like added to smoothies! Most have added nutrients so that approximately 2 tablespoons of the powder supplies at least half the daily recommended amount of protein. My favorite is NutriBiotic Organic Rice Protein because it has the least grainy residue when mixed into smoothies. Also, the rice product is absorbed more slowly and lasts longer than soy protein products. For those allergic to soy, this is the perfect protein powder.

> My favorite protein powder is NutriBiotic Organic Rice Protein because it has the least grainy residue in smoothies.

RAISINS

These add sweetness and some little bits to chew to a smoothie. Raisins are very high in potassium and a good source of carbohydrates.

SUNFLOWER SEEDS

These seeds supply calcium, phosphorus, iron, potassium, thiamine and other trace minerals. They can be used to make "milk" for smoothies. Toasted seeds provide an excellent "crunch" to a smoothie when added during the last few seconds of blending.

TOFU

This concentrated protein made from soy milk comes in a variety of forms. You can buy regular, firm, extra firm, lite and fat-free. It is packaged in liquid, which needs to be refrigerated, or in aseptic boxes which can be stored on the shelf. "Regular" tofu is the creamiest, but it is high in fat. For most smoothies, I use "fat-free." Tofu powder is sold as a milk substitute. It is available in "regular" and "fat-free" and is excellent in smoothies, on cereals, or for drinking.

VITAMIN C

This vital antioxidant has been shown to protect against the dangerous effects of pollution. It promotes wound healing and is essential for tissue growth and repair, proper adrenal gland function, and maintaining healthy gums. Regular use of vitamin C may also reduce cholesterol levels and high blood pressure, and prevent arteriosclerosis.

Regular use of vitamin C may also reduce cholesterol levels and high blood pressure, and prevent arteriosclerosis.

Sources: berries, citrus fruits, broccoli leaves, beet greens, spinach, kale, parsley, green pepper, black currants - note the color!

WHEAT GERM

This is the most nutritious part of the wheatberry, the part that is stripped in milling wheat into white flour. It is rich in B-vitamins, vitamin E, trace minerals and protein. It is a good source of protein & unsaturated fatty acids. Dry wheat germ and wheat germ oil goes rancid quickly, so it should be purchased vacuum packed or refrigerated, kept refrigerated, and should be used before the date stamped on the product.

WHEAT, SPROUTED

Wheat that has been sprouted 3 days, blended with water, then strained, makes a good sweet "milk" (use 1 c. sprouted wheat and 2 cups water). For extra fiber, you can add 1/4 c. of sprouted wheat to a smoothie and blend well. Most people with wheat allergies can tolerate sprouted wheat. If your allergies to wheat are not life-threatening, give it a try!

Note: Rather than adding vitamins and minerals separately, I add Juice Plus+ fruit and/or vegetable juice capsules containing fiber and powdered enzymes to each smoothie to ensure a balanced supply of nutrients and antioxidants to boost the immune system, repair DNA so the body can fight cancer and other degenerative diseases.

The following *starred* supplements are either very strong flavored or dark green in color. They can be added, but use caution on your amounts. Usually, by the time you put *enough* in to be healthful, you've created a zimmy-zommy drink that no one wants to drink, but many people like to add just a LITTLE extra "something" to each drink.

*BARLEY GRASS

Most of the recommended RDA nutrients come from dark green, leafy vegetables. Since most of us don't consume nearly enough, barley grass (or spirulina, liquid chlorophyll, wheat grass) supplies essential amino acids, as well as chlorophyll, enzymes and minerals calcium, iron, and vitamins B_{12} and C. Add to a tomato-based smoothie, or mix with apple juice.

*CHLOROPHYLL

This comes in a liquid, capsule and powdered form. It is similar to barley grass, but slightly different in flavor. I like the brands that add mint so aftertaste is pleasant. Chlorophyll

> Wheat that has been sprouted 3 days, blended with water, then strained, makes a good sweet "milk."

and other green-colored products are good for cleansing and detoxifying the blood. They are excellent sources of minerals, enzymes and other important nutrients such as vitamin A. Because of its dark color and taste, it tastes best when mixed into a pineapple smoothie, but don't count on this one winning any prize for looks!

*GINKGO BILOBA

This herb is widely known as the "intelligent herb" because it has been used successfully in improving memory and in slowing the aging process, including Alzheimer's disease. It is an antioxidant that has been shown to increase the supply of oxygen to the heart and brain, as well as throughout the rest of the body. This is another of the traditional add-ins that can't be added in large enough doses to really do much good.

*GINSENG

For centuries, ginseng has been used throughout the Orient as a tonic for both the mind and the body. Russian scientists have made claims that the ginseng root stimulates physical and mental activity, improves endocrine gland function and has a positive effect on the sex glands. Today it is widely used for fatigue, to enhance athletic performance, and to detoxify the body.

> Ginseng should not be used by those who have problems with hypoglycemia, high blood pressure or heart disorders.

Note: Ginseng should not be used by those who have problems with hypoglycemia, high blood pressure or heart disorders.

Another note: This is one of those add-ins that is touted for its beneficial effects, but I have found that by the time I put enough into a smoothie to get those beneficial effects, I've ruined the great taste of my treat. I suggest you open a few capsules and mix with a small amount of your smoothie and gulp it down, then enjoy the rest! *Or,* swallow the capsules and enjoy it all!

*PRIMROSE OIL

This is another of the fatty acids that has been very helpful in reducing high blood pressure, relieving pain and inflammation, including hot flashes. Again, the flavor is a little hard to get past.

*SPIRULINA

Considered one of the world's superfoods, spirulina has a high content of protein, vitamins, minerals, and other important nutrients. It has been shown to aid in protecting the immune system, lowering cholesterol, and in mineral absorption. Due to its dark green color, a healthy dose of it ruins the visual appeal of a fruit smoothie, but would be good in a tomato-based veggie smoothie. ❤

LIST YOUR FAVORITE SMOOTHIE ADD-INS HERE:

EQUIPMENT TO HAVE ON HAND

- **Heavy Duty Blender**
- **Hand or electric grain grinder***
- **Strainer**

Note: "Milks" called for in this book can be made at home using a hand or electric grain grinder, or purchased at a health food store or co-op. Or, use regular milk or reconstituted powdered milk.

SMOOTHIE SHOPPING CHECKLIST

Add-Ins (my favorites)
- ☐ acidophilus powder
- ☐ aloe vera juice
- ☐ brewer's yeast
- ☐ C-Crystals (vitamin C powder)
- ☐ flaxseed oil-Barlean's
- ☐ liquid chlorophyll
- ☐ Juice Plus+ powdered juice capsules

Flavorings - Sweeteners
- ☐ carob powder
- ☐ coconut extract
- ☐ honey
- ☐ malted milk powder
- ☐ orange extract
- ☐ pecan nut flavoring
- ☐ pure maple syrup
- ☐ rum flavoring - artificial
- ☐ vanilla

Fruits - fresh and/or frozen
- ☐ apples
- ☐ applesauce, unsweetened
- ☐ apricots
- ☐ avocado
- ☐ bananas
- ☐ blackberries
- ☐ blueberries
- ☐ cantaloupe
- ☐ casaba melon
- ☐ honeydew melon
- ☐ kiwi fruit
- ☐ lemon
- ☐ lime
- ☐ mango
- ☐ pineapple
- ☐ pineapple chunks, in juice

- ☐ pineapple, crushed, in juice
- ☐ oranges
- ☐ papayas
- ☐ peaches
- ☐ pears
- ☐ plums
- ☐ red grapes
- ☐ raisins
- ☐ raspberries
- ☐ red apples
- ☐ strawberries
- ☐ watermelon

100% Fruit Juices
- ☐ Black Cherry Juice-Knudsen
- ☐ Apricot Nectar-Knudsen
- ☐ cranberry juice
- ☐ fruit punch
- ☐ fresh-squeezed grapefruit juice
- ☐ lemon juice
- ☐ Vita Juice-Simply Nutritious
- ☐ Pineapple Juice-Del Monte
- ☐ papaya nectar

100% Fruit Juice Concentrates
- ☐ orange juice
- ☐ apple juice
- ☐ grape juice
- ☐ creamed papaya

Dole 100% Fruit Juice Concentrates
- ☐ Country Raspberry
- ☐ Mountain Cherry
- ☐ Pineapple Orange
- ☐ Pineapple-Orange Banana
- ☐ Pineapple-Orange Strawberry
- ☐ Pineapple Juice

Welch's 100% Fruit Juice Concentrates (these 100% juices DO NOT contain sulfites)

- ☐ White Grape
- ☐ White Grape Cranberry
- ☐ White Grape Peach
- ☐ White Grape Raspberry

100% Fruit Spreads

- ☐ blueberry
- ☐ apricot
- ☐ strawberry

Grains - Flours
(Use these to make your own milks)

- ☐ brown rice
- ☐ barley, whole
- ☐ oats (oat groats)
- ☐ oat flour-Arrowhead Mills
- ☐ barley flour-Arrowhead Mills

Milks - Non-Dairy (liquid or powder)

- ☐ almond milk-Pacific Foods
- ☐ oat milk
- ☐ Better Than Milk®, light
  - ☐ vanilla, ☐ plain, ☐ soy
- ☐ soy beverage, non fat-WestSoy
- ☐ Rice Dream®
- ☐ rice milk, fat free, plain
- ☐ soy milk, regular, lite or fat-free
- ☐ Rice Moo™-Sovex
- ☐ Soy Moo®-Health Valley

Nuts, Nut Butters - Seeds

- ☐ almonds and almond butter
- ☐ peanut butter
- ☐ sesame seeds, unhulled
- ☐ sunflower seeds, raw
- ☐ tahini (sesame butter)

Protein Powders

- ☐ Nature's Life Pro-Life Soy
- ☐ Nutribiotic® Organic Rice
- ☐ Naturade® Vegetable

Seasonings - Spices

- ☐ Better Than Bouillon®- Superior Touch Vegetarian Vegetable
- ☐ black pepper
- ☐ cinnamon
- ☐ HerbOx bouillons - without MSG
- ☐ nutmeg
- ☐ sea salt
- ☐ tabasco sauce
- ☐ worcestershire sauce

Tofu

- ☐ any brand - choose from low-fat or regular
- ☐ lite tofu, firm-Mori-nu (my favorite)

Vegetable Juices

- ☐ raw beet juice
- ☐ raw carrot juice, organic
- ☐ raw celery juice
- ☐ raw mixed vegetable juices
- ☐ V-8® vegetable juice

Vegetables

- ☐ carrots
- ☐ beets
- ☐ ginger root
- ☐ mint leaves
- ☐ parsley
- ☐ pumpkin, canned
- ☐ red or green bell pepper
- ☐ spinach leaves - fresh or frozen
- ♥

BERRY GOOD SMOOTHIES

Berry Delightful and Berry Delicious!

I grew up in Gresham, Oregon (berry country), so I love the taste (and extra fiber of the seeds) berries add to smoothies. Berries are dark in color, indicating higher nutrient values than those in light fruits such as white grapes, apples or bananas.

Blackberries, which grow wild and quickly to take over any untended ground, are a good source of calcium, potassium, vitamin A and vitamin C. Blueberries and raspberries contain small amounts of nearly all nutrients. Strawberries are high in vitamin C.

RED RASPBERRY

2 c. oat milk
1 t. vanilla
1/2 c. Dole Country Raspberry concentrate
1 c. frozen raspberries
1 frozen banana
10 ice cubes

 Place oat milk (or your choice of any other milk or non-dairy substitute) and all remaining ingredients in blender in order given. (If adding protein powder, add first and blend with liquid.)

 Add one or two of the following per serving (opt.):
1/2 T. rice protein powder
1 1/2 t. flaxseed oil
1/4 t. acidophilus powder
1/8 t. vitamin C powder

 Blend until smooth and creamy. For thickest smoothies, keep blending time to a minimum.

Makes 6 cups. Serves 4. Serving Size 12 oz.

Calories	129
Fat	.5g
Carbohydrate	30.6g
Protein	1.6g
Potassium	286mg
Vitamin C	42mg
Fiber	3.1g

RASPBERRY TOFU SHAKE

1 c. oat milk
2/3 c. Dole Country Raspberry concentrate
12 oz. pkg. firm lite tofu
2 frozen bananas
8 ice cubes

Place oat milk (or your choice of any other milk or non-dairy substitute) and all remaining ingredients in blender in order given. (If nuts are added, add during the last few seconds of blending for a crunchy texture.)

Add one or two of the following per serving (opt.):
1 1/2 t. flaxseed oil
1/4 t. acidophilus powder
1 T. toasted nuts

Blend until smooth and creamy.

Makes 4 1/2 cups. Serves 3. Serving Size 12 oz.

Calories	246
Fat	1.9g
Carbohydrate	51.6g
Protein	8.7g
Potassium	507mg
Vitamin C	61mg
Fiber	2.1g

NANABERRY SHAKE

1 c. barley milk
2/3 c. apple juice concentrate
1 t. vanilla
2 frozen bananas
6 large strawberries
6 ice cubes

Place barley milk (or your choice of any other milk or non-dairy substitute) and all remaining ingredients in blender in order given. (If adding protein powder, add first and blend with liquid.)

Add one or two of the following per serving (opt.):
1/2 T. rice protein powder
1 1/2 t. flaxseed oil
1-2 t. lecithin granules
1/8 t. vitamin C powder

Blend until smooth and creamy. For thickest smoothies, keep blending time to a minimum.

Makes 4 1/2 cups. Serves 3. Serving Size 12 oz.

Calories	234
Fat	.6g
Carbohydrate	56.1g
Protein	2.4g
Potassium	680mg
Vitamin C	98mg
Fiber	4.6g

STRAWBERRY FRAPPÉ

2/3 c. oat milk
1 c. pineapple juice
2/3 c. apple juice concentrate
1/2 t. vanilla
6 large frozen strawberries
10 ice cubes

 Place oat milk (or your choice of any other milk or non-dairy substitute) and all remaining ingredients in blender in order given. (If adding protein powder, add first and blend with liquid.)

 Add one or two of the following per serving (opt.):
1/2 T. protein powder
1 1/2 t. flaxseed oil
1/4 t. acidophilus powder
1-2 t. wheat germ

 Blend until smooth and creamy. For thickest smoothies, keep blending time to a minimum.

Makes 4 1/2 cups. Serves 3. Serving Size 12 oz.

Calories 164
Fat 3g
Carbohydrate .. 40g
Protein 8g
Potassium 432mg
Vitamin C 112mg
Fiber 2g

BLACKBERRY HI-PRO FREEZE

1 T. raw sunflower seeds, ground to a fine meal
2 c. oat milk
1/2 c. frozen apple juice concentrate
1 t. vanilla
1 c. frozen blackberries
1 frozen banana
10 ice cubes

 Place oat milk (or your choice of any other milk or non-dairy substitute) and all remaining ingredients in blender in order given. (If adding protein powder, add first and blend with liquid.)

 Add one or two of the following per serving (opt.):
1/2 T. rice protein powder
1/4 t. acidophilus powder
1/8 t. vitamin C powder

 Blend until smooth and creamy. For thickest smoothies, keep blending time to a minimum.

Makes 6 cups. Serves 4. Serving Size 12 oz.

Calories	164
Fat	1.6g
Carbohydrate	37.1g
Protein	2g
Potassium	439mg
Vitamin C	43mg
Fiber	3.7g

CREAMY STRAWBERRY

2 c. barley milk
1 t. vanilla
1 c. frozen apple juice concentrate
1 c. frozen strawberries
1 frozen banana

Place barley milk (or your choice of any other milk or non-dairy substitute) and all remaining ingredients in blender in order given. (If adding protein powder, add first and blend with liquid.)

Add one or two of the following per serving (opt.):
1/2 T. rice protein powder
1 1/2 t. flaxseed oil
1/4 t. acidophilus powder
1-2 T. chopped dates

Blend until smooth and creamy. For thickest smoothies, keep blending time to a minimum.

Makes 6 cups. Serves 4. Serving Size 12 oz.

Calories	259
Fat	.2g
Carbohydrate	62.6g
Protein	2.6g
Potassium	643mg
Vitamin C	76mg
Fiber	5.3g

BERRY BLUEBERRY MALT

6 almonds
2 c. barley milk
1 1/2 t. vanilla
2 T. malted milk powder
1 c. frozen apple juice concentrate
1 1/4 c. frozen blueberries
1 1/2 frozen bananas

 Place barley milk (or your choice of any other milk or non-dairy substitute) and all remaining ingredients in blender in order given.

 Add one or two of the following per serving (opt.):
1 1/2 t. flaxseed oil
1/4 t. acidophilus powder
1/8 t. vitamin C powder

 Blend almonds and barley milk until smooth and creamy. Add remaining ingredients and blend until smooth.

Makes 6 cups. Serves 4. Serving Size 12 oz.

Calories	311
Fat	3.6g
Carbohydrate	66.2g
Protein	4.5g
Potassium	643mg
Vitamin C	76mg
Fiber	5.3g

BANANA BERRY MALT

1 c. water
1/4 c. barley milk
3 frozen bananas
8 large frozen strawberries
3 T. malted milk powder (opt.)

1 t. lemon juice
2/3 c. apple juice concentrate
8 ice cubes

 Place barley milk (or your choice of any other milk or non-dairy substitute) and all remaining ingredients in blender in order given. (If adding protein powder, add first and blend with liquid.)

 Add one or two of the following per serving (opt.):
1/2 T. rice protein powder
1 1/2 t. flaxseed oil
1/4 t. acidophilus powder
1-2 t. wheat germ

 Blend until smooth and creamy.

Makes 6 cups. Serves 4. Serving Size 12 oz.

Calories 564
Fat 1.2g
Carbohydrate .. 148g
Protein 3.8g
Potassium 1043mg
Vitamin C 55mg
Fiber 4.1g

BERRY GOOD SMOOTHIES

CREAMY BANANA-BLACKBERRY

1/2 c. oat milk
1/3 c. frozen apple juice concentrate
1 t. vanilla
1/2 c. lite tofu
2/3 c. frozen blackberries
1 frozen banana
6 ice cubes

 Place oat milk (or your choice of any other milk or non-dairy substitute) and all remaining ingredients in blender in order given.

 Add one or two of the following per serving (opt.):
1 T. raisins
1 1/2 t. flaxseed oil
1/4 t. acidophilus powder
1/8 t. vitamin C powder

 Blend until smooth and creamy.

Makes 3 cups. Serves 2. Serving Size 12 oz.

Calories	197
Fat	1.4g
Carbohydrate	42.9g
Protein	5.2g
Potassium	501mg
Vitamin C	55mg
Fiber	4.1g

RASPBERRY FREEZE

1/2 c. oat milk
1 1/2 c. cold water
3/4 c. frozen apple juice concentrate
1 t. vanilla
1/2 c. tofu
1 c. frozen raspberries
1 frozen banana
6 ice cubes

 Place oat milk (or your choice of any other milk or non-dairy substitute) and all remaining ingredients in blender in order given.

 Add one or two of the following per serving (opt.):
1/2 T. oat bran
1 1/2 t. flaxseed oil
1/4 t. acidophilus powder
1/8 t. vitamin C powder

Blend until smooth and creamy.

Makes 3 cups. Serves 2. Serving Size 12 oz.

Calories 308
Fat 2.6g
Carbohydrate . . 66.7g
Protein 5.9g
Potassium 771mg
Vitamin C 128mg
Fiber 5.7g

RAZZLEBERRY

1/2 c. barley milk
1/2 c. apple juice concentrate
1/2 c. frozen red grapes
1 c. frozen raspberries
1 frozen banana

 Place barley milk (or your choice of any other milk or non-dairy substitute) and all remaining ingredients in blender in order given. (If adding protein powder, add first and blend with liquid.)

 Add one or two of the following per serving (opt.):
1/2 T. rice protein powder
1 1/2 t. flaxseed oil
1/4 t. acidophilus powder
1/8 t. vitamin C powder

 Blend until smooth and creamy. For thickest smoothies, keep blending time to a minimum.

Makes 4 1/2 cups. Serves 3. Serving Size 12 oz.

Calories 172
Fat 4g
Carbohydrate .. 42.3g
Protein 1.4g
Potassium 483mg
Vitamin C 61mg
Fiber 5.1g

RAZZLEPEAR

2/3 c. soy milk
1/4 c. Dole Country Raspberry concentrate
3 ripe pears, cored
12 ice cubes

Place soy milk (or your choice of any other milk or non-dairy substitute) and all remaining ingredients in blender in order given. (If adding protein powder, add first and blend with liquid.)

Add one or two of the following per serving (opt.):
1/2 T. rice protein powder
1 1/2 t. flaxseed oil
1/4 t. acidophilus powder
1/8 t. vitamin C powder

Blend until smooth and creamy. For thickest smoothies, keep blending time to a minimum.

Makes 4 1/2 cups. Serves 3. Serving Size 12 oz.

Calories	162
Fat	1.7g
Carbohydrate	37.4g
Protein	2.5g
Potassium	356mg
Vitamin C	27mg
Fiber	4.7g

BLACKBERRY NANNA

1 1/2 c. water
1/2 c. barley milk
1/2 c. apple juice concentrate
1/2 t. vanilla
2 frozen bananas
2/3 c. frozen blackberries

 Place barley milk (or your choice of any other milk or non-dairy substitute) and all remaining ingredients in blender in order given. (If adding protein powder, add first and blend with liquid.)

 Add one or two of the following per serving (opt.):
1/2 T. rice protein powder
1 1/2 t. flaxseed oil
1/4 t. acidophilus powder
1/8 t. vitamin C powder

 Blend until smooth and creamy. For thickest smoothies, keep blending time to a minimum.

Makes 4 1/2 cups. Serves 3. Serving Size 12 oz.

Calories	192
Fat	.5g
Carbohydrate	46.8g
Protein	1.9g
Potassium	562mg
Vitamin C	55mg
Fiber	4.3g

CAROB RASPBERRY

1/2 c. water
1/2 c. barley milk
1 T. carob powder
3/4 c. apple juice concentrate
1 c. frozen raspberries
1 1/4 frozen bananas
12 ice cubes

 Place barley milk (or your choice of any other milk or non-dairy substitute) and all remaining ingredients in blender in order given.

 Add one or two of the following per serving (opt.):
1-2 t. lecithin granules
1 1/2 t. flaxseed oil
1/4 t. acidophilus powder
1/8 t. vitamin C powder

 Blend only until smooth and creamy.

Makes 4 1/2 cups. Serves 3. Serving Size 12 oz.

Calories 207
Fat 5g
Carbohydrate . . 51.3g
Protein 1.6g
Potassium 563mg
Vitamin C 85mg
Fiber 5g

BLACKBERRY BREEZE

1 c. oat milk
1/2 c. frozen apple juice concentrate
1/2 t. vanilla
1 frozen banana
1/2 c. frozen blackberries
1/2" slice firm lite tofu
6 ice cubes

 Place oat milk (or your choice of any other milk or non-dairy substitute) and all remaining ingredients in blender in order given.

 Add one or two of the following per serving (opt.):
1 T. sunflower seeds
1 1/2 t. flaxseed oil
1/4 t. acidophilus powder
1/8 t. vitamin C powder

 Blend until smooth and creamy. For thickest smoothies, keep blending time to a minimum.

Makes 3 cups. Serves 2. Serving Size 12 oz.

Calories	220
Fat	.9g
Carbohydrate	51.5g
Protein	2.8g
Potassium	591mg
Vitamin C	79mg
Fiber	3.6g

CITRUS SMOOTHIES

Extra Vitamin C for an immune system boost!

Building a strong immune system is important, and what a yummy way to take your vitamins! Oranges assist in correcting overacidic body conditions and help a sluggish intestinal tract start movin' along! Grapefruits are rich in potassium and calcium, helping to promote a sound sleep when eaten at night.

ORANGE JULIUS

1 cup water
1 T. Better Than Milk tofu powder
1/2 t. vanilla
1/2 c. Welch's 100% White Grape juice concentrate
3/4 c. orange juice concentrate
12 ice cubes

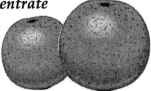

 Place water (or your choice of any milk or non-dairy substitute) and all remaining ingredients in blender in order given.

 Add one or two of the following per serving (opt.):
1 1/2 t. flaxseed oil
1/4 t. acidophilus powder
1/8 t. vitamin C powder

 Blend just until ice is fine.

Makes 3 cups. Serves 2. Serving Size 12 oz.

Calories	361
Fat	1.5g
Carbohydrate	84.7g
Protein	3g
Potassium	735mg
Vitamin C	119mg
Fiber	.8g

CITRUS  **SMOOTHIES**

ORANGE BANANA CREME

1/2 c. water
1/2 c. orange juice concentrate
1/4 c. Welch's 100% White Grape juice concentrate
3 T. Better Than Milk tofu powder
1/2 t. vanilla
1/2 frozen banana
12 ice cubes (or enough to make slushy)

Place water (or your choice of any milk or non-dairy substitute) and all remaining ingredients in blender in order given. (If adding protein powder, add first and blend with liquid.)

Add one or two of the following per serving (opt.):
1 T. almonds
1 1/2 t. flaxseed oil
1/4 t. acidophilus powder
1/8 t. vitamin C powder

Blend until smooth and creamy. If almonds are used, add during last few seconds of blending.

Makes 3 cups. Serves 2. Serving Size 12 oz.

Calories	292
Fat	4.1g
Carbohydrate	62.1g
Protein	3.5g
Potassium	644mg
Vitamin C	70mg
Fiber	1.2g

CHERRY LIMEADE

3/4 c. water
2/3 c. barley milk
1/2 c. Dole Mountain Cherry concentrate
1/2 c. apple juice concentrate
1 fresh lime, peeled
14 ice cubes

Place barley milk (or your choice of any other milk or non-dairy substitute) and all remaining ingredients in blender in order given.

Add one or two of the following per serving (opt.):
1 1/2 t. flaxseed oil
1/4 t. acidophilus powder

Blend until smooth. For thickest smoothies, keep blending time to a minimum.

Makes 4 1/2 cups. Serves 3. Serving Size 12 oz.

Calories	135
Fat	.1g
Carbohydrate	32.8g
Protein	1.2g
Potassium	305mg
Vitamin C	67mg
Fiber	1.8g

CITRUS SMOOTHIES

LIME FREEZE

1/2 c. water
1/2 c. barley milk
2/3 c. Welch's 100% White Grape Juice concentrate
1/2 c. Dole Pineapple Orange juice concentrate
1/2 of a fresh lime, peeled
1-2 frozen bananas
16 ice cubes

 Place barley milk (or your choice of any other milk or non-dairy substitute) and all remaining ingredients in blender in order given.

 Add one or two of the following per serving (opt.):
1 1/2 t. flaxseed oil
1/4 t. acidophilus powder

 Blend until smooth. For thickest smoothies, keep blending time to a minimum.

Makes 6 cups. Serves 4. Serving Size 12 oz.

Calories	242
Fat	.3g
Carbohydrate	59.7g
Protein	1.7g
Potassium	421mg
Vitamin C	85mg
Fiber	2.2g

BREAKFAST EYE OPENER

1/2 c. water
2/3 c. barley milk
1/2 c. Dole Pineapple Orange juice concentrate
1/3 c. freshly squeezed grapefruit juice, with pulp
1 frozen banana
4 ice cubes

Place barley milk (or your choice of any other milk or non-dairy substitute) and all remaining ingredients in blender in order given.

Add one or two of the following per serving (opt.):
1 t. brewer's yeast
1 1/2 t. flaxseed oil
1/4 t. acidophilus powder

Blend until smooth. For thickest smoothies, keep blending time to a minimum.

Makes 3 cups. Serves 2. Serving Size 12 oz.

Calories	229
Fat	.3g
Carbohydrate	54.9g
Protein	3.1g
Potassium	672mg
Vitamin C	80mg
Fiber	3g

PINK GRAPEFRUIT

1 c. oat milk
1/2 c. Dole Mountain Cherry concentrate
1/3 c. freshly squeezed grapefruit juice, with pulp
1 frozen banana
6 ice cubes

Place oat milk (or your choice of any other milk or non-dairy substitute) and all remaining ingredients in blender in order given.

Add one or two of the following per serving (opt.):
1-2 t. wheat germ
1 1/2 t. flaxseed oil
1/4 t. acidophilus powder

Blend until smooth. For thickest smoothies, keep blending time to a minimum.

Makes 3 cups. Serves 2. Serving Size 12 oz.

Calories 115
Fat 5g
Carbohydrate .. 27.6g
Protein 1.5g
Potassium 395mg
Vitamin C 40mg
Fiber 1.7g

CITRUS SPECIAL

1/3 c. freshly squeezed grapefruit juice, with pulp
2 c. Del Monte canned pineapple juice
1/2 c. orange juice concentrate
1/2 c. lite tofu
1 frozen banana
6 ice cubes

Place ingredients in blender in order given.

Add one or two of the following per serving (opt.):
1 1/2 t. flaxseed oil
1/4 t. acidophilus powder
1/8 t. vitamin C powder

Blend until smooth.

Makes 4 1/2 cups. Serves 3. Serving Size 12 oz.

Calories	208
Fat	.8g
Carbohydrate	49g
Protein	4.8g
Potassium	672mg
Vitamin C	75mg
Fiber	2.6g

LEMON CREME SUPREME

1 c. water
3/4 c. Dole 100% Pineapple Orange Juice concentrate
1 lemon - juice and pulp
1/2 c. lite firm tofu
1 frozen banana
4-8 ice cubes

 Place ingredients in blender in order given. (If adding protein powder, add first and blend with liquid.)

 Add one or two of the following per serving (opt.):
1/2 T. rice protein powder
1 1/2 t. flaxseed oil
1/4 t. acidophilus powder

 Blend until smooth and creamy. For thickest smoothies, keep blending time to a minimum.

Makes 4 1/2 cups. Serves 3. Serving Size 12 oz.

Calories 176
Fat 8g
Carbohydrate . . 41.9g
Protein 4.3g
Potassium 549mg
Vitamin C 91mg
Fiber 9g

CITRUS 🍊 **SMOOTHIES**   *Page 55*

PEACHY ORANGE

1/2 c. water
1/2 c. barley milk
1/2 c. orange juice concentrate
1/4 c. Welch's 100% White Grape Peach concentrate
2 frozen bananas
1/4 c. firm tofu

Place barley milk (or your choice of any other milk or non-dairy substitute) and all remaining ingredients in blender in order given.

Add one or two of the following per serving (opt.):
1 1/2 t. flaxseed oil
1/4 c. aloe vera juice
1/4 t. acidophilus powder
1/8 t. vitamin C powder

Blend until smooth and creamy. For thickest smoothies, keep blending time to a minimum.

Makes 3 cups. Serves 2. Serving Size 12 oz.

Calories	338
Fat	1.2g
Carbohydrate	79.4g
Protein	6.4g
Potassium	956mg
Vitamin C	77mg
Fiber	4.5g

CITRUS  **SMOOTHIES**

BANANA BERRY CREME

1/2 c. water
1/2 c. barley milk
1/2 c. orange juice concentrate
1/4 c. Welch's 100% White Grape Peach concentrate
1/4 c. Polaner All Fruit Apricot jam
1/4 c. firm lite tofu
8 frozen strawberries
2 frozen bananas

Place barley milk (or your choice of any other milk or non-dairy substitute) and all remaining ingredients in blender in order given.

This smoothie is high in calories, many of which come from *simple carbohydrates*, so don't enjoy this one too often!

Add one or two of the following per serving (opt.):
1-2 T. chopped dates
1 1/2 t. flaxseed oil
1/4 t. acidophilus powder

Blend until smooth and creamy. For thickest smoothies, keep blending time to a minimum.

Makes 3 cups. Serves 2. Serving Size 12 oz.

Calories 453
Fat 1.4g
Carbohydrate . . 110g
Protein 6.4g
Potassium 1110mg
Vitamin C 123mg
Fiber 6.7g

ORANGE PEACH DELITE

1/2 c. water
1/2 c. barley milk
2 T. Natureade Vegetable Protein powder
1/2 c. orange juice concentrate
1/4 c. Polaner All Fruit Apricot jam
1/4 c. frozen peach dices
1 frozen banana
4 ice cubes

Place water and protein powder in blender and process until smooth. Add remaining ingredients to blender in order given.

Add one or two of the following per serving (opt.):
1 1/2 t. flaxseed oil
1/4 t. acidophilus powder
1/8 t. vitamin C powder

Blend until smooth and creamy. For thickest smoothies, keep blending time to a minimum.

Makes 3 cups. Serves 2. Serving Size 12 oz.

Calories	162
Fat	.3g
Carbohydrate	53.9g
Protein	7.9g
Potassium	524mg
Vitamin C	26mg
Fiber	2.5g

CITRUS  **SMOOTHIES**

PEACHYNANNA

1/2 c. water
2 T. Natureade Vegetable Protein powder
1/2 c. barley milk
1/2 c. orange juice concentrate
1/4 c. apple juice concentrate
1/3 c. Polaner All Fruit Apricot jam
1 t. vanilla

1/3 c. frozen peach dices
3 frozen bananas
4 ice cubes

Place water and protein powder in blender and process until smooth. Add remaining ingredients to blender in order given.

Add one or two of the following per serving (opt.):
1 T. almonds
1 1/2 t. flaxseed oil
1/4 t. acidophilus powder
1/8 t. vitamin C powder

Blend until smooth and creamy. For thickest smoothies, keep blending time to a minimum.

Makes 4 1/2 cups. Serves 3. Serving Size 12 oz.

Calories 273
Fat 7g
Carbohydrate .. 61.4g
Protein 8.7g
Potassium 923mg
Vitamin C 56mg
Fiber 4.3g

"BERRY" PEACHY

1/2 c. water
1/2 c. barley milk
2 T. Natureade Vegetable Protein powder
1/2 c. orange juice concentrate
1/4 c. apple juice concentrate
1/4 c. frozen peach pieces
1/4 c. frozen raspberries
1 frozen banana
4 ice cubes

Place water, barley milk and protein powder in blender and process until smooth. Add remaining ingredients to blender in order given.

Add one or two of the following per serving (opt.):
1 1/2 t. flaxseed oil
1 T. sprouted wheat
1/4 t. acidophilus powder
1/8 t. vitamin C powder

Blend until smooth and creamy. For thickest smoothies, keep blending time to a minimum.

Makes 3 cups. Serves 2. Serving Size 12 oz.

Calories	274
Fat	3.4g
Carbohydrate	61.4g
Protein	4.1g
Potassium	1027mg
Vitamin C	63mg
Fiber	4.1g

CITRUS  **SMOOTHIES**

GOLDEN BREAKFAST

1/4 c. water
1/2 c. barley milk
2 T. Natureade Vegetable Protein powder
1/2 t. vanilla
1/4 c. apple juice concentrate
1/2 c. orange juice concentrate
1/4 c. frozen avocado chunks
1 c. frozen peach pieces
6 ice cubes

Place water, barley milk and protein powder in blender and process until smooth. Add remaining ingredients to blender in order given.

Add one or two of the following per serving (opt.):
1 1/2 t. flaxseed oil
1 t. brewer's yeast
1/4 t. acidophilus powder
1/8 t. vitamin C powder

Blend until smooth and creamy. For thickest smoothies, keep blending time to a minimum.

Makes 3 cups. Serves 2. Serving Size 12 oz.

Calories	321
Fat	4.6g
Carbohydrate	60.3g
Protein	12.2g
Potassium	993mg
Vitamin C	75mg
Fiber	5.2g

CITRUS SMOOTHIES

ORANGE APRICOT SOOTHER

1 c. oat milk
1/2 c. Dole Pineapple Orange concentrate
1/4 c. Polaner All Fruit Apricot Jam
1/2 c. peeled orange slices
2 frozen bananas
8 ice cubes

 Place oat milk (or your choice of any other milk or non-dairy substitute) and all remaining ingredients in blender in order given. (If adding protein powder, add first and blend with liquid.)

 Add one or two of the following per serving (opt.):
1/2 T. rice protein powder
1 1/2 t. flaxseed oil
1/4 t. acidophilus powder
1/8 t. vitamin C powder

 Blend until smooth and creamy. For thickest smoothies, keep blending time to a minimum.

Makes 4 1/2 cups. Serves 3. Serving Size 12 oz.

Calories	174
Fat	.6g
Carbohydrate	42.6g
Protein	2.1g
Potassium	596mg
Vitamin C	63mg
Fiber	2.8g

CITRUS  SMOOTHIES

APRICOT CREME

1 c. oat milk
2 T. orange juice concentrate
1/2 c. Dole Pineapple Orange concentrate
1/4 c. Polaner All Fruit Apricot Jam
1 frozen banana
12 ice cubes

 Place oat milk (or your choice of any other milk or non-dairy substitute) and all remaining ingredients in blender in order given. (If adding protein powder, add first and blend with liquid.)

 Add one or two of the following per serving (opt.):
1/2 T. rice protein powder
1 1/2 t. flaxseed oil
1/4 t. acidophilus powder
1/8 t. vitamin C powder

 Blend until smooth and creamy. For thickest smoothies, keep blending time to a minimum.

Makes 4 1/2 cups. Serves 3. Serving Size 12 oz.

Calories	144
Fat	.4g
Carbohydrate	34.7g
Protein	1.7g
Potassium	471mg
Vitamin C	49mg
Fiber	1.2g

CREAMY ORANGE

1/2 c. water
1/2 c. barley milk
3/4 c. orange juice concentrate
1/2 t. lemon juice
1" slice lite tofu
6 ice cubes

Place barley milk (or your choice of any other milk or non-dairy substitute) and all remaining ingredients in blender in order given. (If adding protein powder, add first and blend with liquid.)

Add one or two of the following per serving (opt.):
1/2 T. rice protein powder
1 1/2 t. flaxseed oil
1/4 t. acidophilus powder
1 T. sunflower seeds

Blend until smooth and creamy. For thickest smoothies, keep blending time to a minimum.

Makes 3 cups. Serves 2. Serving Size 12 oz.

Calories	216
Fat	.7g
Carbohydrate	48.2g
Protein	6g
Potassium	745mg
Vitamin C	49mg
Fiber	2.1g

MORNING SUNRISE

What a great way to start the day! The colorful blend of orange, apple, grape, and pineapple juices produces a refreshing drink -- at breakfast or ANY time.

1/2 c. Knudsen's Vita Juice
1/4 c. orange juice concentrate
1/4 c. apple juice concentrate
1/2 c. lite soy milk
12 ice cubes

Place soy milk (or your choice of any other milk or non-dairy substitute) and all remaining ingredients in blender in order given. (If adding protein powder, add first and blend with liquid.)

Add one or two of the following per serving (opt.):
1/2 T. rice protein powder
1/2 T. oat bran
1/4 t. acidophilus powder
1/8 t. vitamin C powder

Blend until smooth and creamy. For thickest smoothies, keep blending time to a minimum.

Makes 3 cups. Serves 2. Serving Size 12 oz.

Calories 165
Fat 1g
Carbohydrate . . 38.9g
Protein 2.1g
Potassium 441mg
Vitamin C 66mg
Fiber 5g

CITRUS 🍊 **SMOOTHIES**

LEMON JULIUS

1 1/2 c. soy milk
1 c. apple juice concentrate
1 small lemon - peeled and seeded
1/2" slice tofu (opt.)
20 ice cubes

Place soy milk (or your choice of any other milk or non-dairy substitute) and all remaining ingredients in blender in order given. (If adding protein powder, add first and blend with liquid.)

Add one or two of the following per serving (opt.):
1/2 T. rice protein powder
1 1/2 t. flaxseed oil
1/4 t. acidophilus powder
1/8 t. vitamin C powder

Blend until smooth and creamy. For thickest smoothies, keep blending time to a minimum.

Makes 4 1/2 cups. Serves 3. Serving Size 12 oz.

Calories 204
Fat 1g
Carbohydrate .. 49.9g
Protein 1.9g
Potassium 447mg
Vitamin C 123mg
Fiber 5g

CITRUS ⊜ SMOOTHIES

KIWI LIME-A-NANNA

1/2 c. soy milk
1/2 c. apple juice concentrate
2 kiwi, peeled
1/2" slice firm lite tofu
1 frozen banana
4 ice cubes

Place soy milk (or your choice of any other milk or non-dairy substitute) and all remaining ingredients in blender in order given.

Add one or two of the following per serving (opt.):
1 1/2 t. flaxseed oil
1/4 t. acidophilus powder
1-2 t. lecithin granules
1/8 t. vitamin C powder

Blend until smooth and creamy. For thickest smoothies, keep blending time to a minimum.

Makes 3 cups. Serves 2. Serving Size 12 oz.

Calories	252
Fat	.9g
Carbohydrate	59.2g
Protein	3.5g
Potassium	813mg
Vitamin C	162mg
Fiber	4.6g

ORANGE BANANA

1/2 c. water
1/2 c. oat milk
2 T. Better Than Milk tofu powder
1/2 c. frozen strawberries
2 frozen bananas
1/2 c. orange juice concentrate

Place water, oat milk (or your choice of any other milk or non-dairy substitute) and tofu powder in blender and process until smooth. Add remaining ingredients.

Add one or two of the following per serving (opt.):
1/2 T. rice protein powder
1 1/2 t. flaxseed oil
1/4 t. acidophilus powder
1/8 t. vitamin C powder

Blend until smooth and creamy. For thickest smoothies, keep blending time to a minimum.

Makes 3 cups. Serves 2. Serving Size 12 oz.

Calories	274
Fat	3.4g
Carbohydrate	61.4g
Protein	4.1g
Potassium	1027mg
Vitamin C	63mg
Fiber	4.1g

CITRUS  **SMOOTHIES**

DECADENT
SMOOTHIES

Delicious drinks for those who need a
"sweet something" for dessert

When I had my first "store bought" smoothie and checked out the ingredient list for the smoothies offered, I recognized that they were all "decadent" by my standards because they were mostly sugared juice concentrates and ice...with a little fruit and teeny tiny amounts of added nutrients. I make smoothies so I can blend in as much fruit as possible, and as many wholesome nutrients as possible and still have an enjoyable drink.

My husband loves all the smoothies in this book, but he grew up with a bigger sweet tooth than the rest of us, so he especially appreciates this section of drinks that don't HAVE to have a full day's supply of fruits and nutrients...they're just plain delicious!

CLAIR'S RICE PUDDING

1 c. barley milk
2 t. vanilla
2 T. raisins
3 T. very light honey or turbinado sugar
1/8 t. cinnamon
1/4 t. nutmeg
dash salt
12 ice cubes

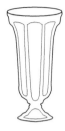

 Place barley milk (or your choice of any other milk or non-dairy substitute) and all remaining ingredients in blender in order given. (If adding protein powder, add first and blend with liquid.)

 Add one or two of the following per serving (opt.):
1/2 T. rice protein powder
1 1/2 t. flaxseed oil
1/4 t. acidophilus powder
1/8 t. vitamin C powder

 Blend until smooth and creamy. For thickest smoothies, keep blending time to a minimum.

Makes 3 cups. Serves 2. Serving Size 12 oz.

Calories 193
Fat 2g
Carbohydrate . . 47.9g
Protein 2.4g
Potassium 138mg
Vitamin C 0mg
Fiber 3g

BANANA NOG

1 c. almond milk
2 c. ice water
1/2 c. Better Than Milk tofu powder
3 T. light honey
3/4 t. vanilla
1/4 t. pecan nut flavoring
dash salt
pinch nutmeg
1 frozen banana

Place almond milk (or your choice of any other milk or non-dairy substitute) and all remaining ingredients in blender in order given.

Add one or two of the following per serving (opt.):
1 1/2 t. flaxseed oil
1/4 t. acidophilus powder
1 T. sunflower seeds
1/8 t. vitamin C powder

Blend until smooth and creamy. For thickest smoothies, keep blending time to a minimum.

Makes 4 1/2 cups. Serves 3. Serving Size 12 oz.

Calories	692
Fat	5.2g
Carbohydrate	149.5g
Protein	11.4g
Potassium	485mg
Vitamin C	10mg
Fiber	2.9g

DECADENT SMOOTHIES

ELVIS PRESLEY SPECIAL

1 1/2 c. barley milk
1/3 c. apple juice concentrate
2 T. peanut butter - low fat
1/2 t. vanilla
1 frozen banana
12 ice cubes

 Place barley milk (or your choice of any other milk or non-dairy substitute) and all remaining ingredients in blender in order given. (If adding protein powder, add first and blend with liquid.) (To reduce the fat of "real" non-homogenized peanut butter, pour oil off top and stir well.)

 Add one or two of the following per serving (opt.):
1/2 T. rice protein powder
1 1/2 t. flaxseed oil
1 T. sunflower seeds
1/8 t. vitamin C powder

 If using chunky peanut butter, add last and blend just until mixed.

Makes 3 cups. Serves 2. Serving Size 12 oz.

Calories	322
Fat	8.4g
Carbohydrate	57g
Protein	8g
Potassium	617mg
Vitamin C	52mg
Fiber	6g

CREAMY PUMPKIN PIE

1 c. low fat soy milk
1/2 c. apple juice concentrate
1/3 c. canned pumpkin
1/4 t. cinnamon
1/2 t. vanilla
dash nutmeg
1/2 frozen banana
6 ice cubes

Place soy milk (or your choice of any other milk or non-dairy substitute) and all remaining ingredients in blender in order given. (If adding protein powder, add first and blend with liquid.)

Add one or two of the following per serving (opt.):
1/2 T. rice protein powder
1 1/2 t. flaxseed oil
1 T. almonds
1/4 t. acidophilus powder

Blend until smooth and creamy. If desired, add optional nuts last for "crunch."

Makes 3 cups. Serves 2. Serving Size 12 oz.

```
Calories  . . . . . . . 201
Fat . . . . . . . . . . . . .3g
Carbohydrate  . . 46.9g
Protein  . . . . . . . . 2.2g
Potassium  . . . . . 495mg
Vitamin C  . . . . . 75mg
Fiber  . . . . . . . . . . 2.5g
```

DECADENT 🥤 SMOOTHIES

FRUIT CREME

1 c. oat milk
1/2 c. Dole Pineapple Orange concentrate
1/4 c. Polaner All Fruit Apricot Jam
1/2 c. frozen raspberries
1 1/2 bananas
12 ice cubes

 Place oat milk (or your choice of any other milk or non-dairy substitute) and all remaining ingredients in blender in order given. (If adding protein powder, add first and blend with liquid.)

 Add one or two of the following per serving (opt.):
1/2 T. rice protein powder
1 1/2 t. flaxseed oil
1/4 t. acidophilus powder
1/8 t. vitamin C powder

 Blend until smooth and creamy. For thickest smoothies, keep blending time to a minimum.

Makes 3 cups. Serves 2. Serving Size 12 oz.

Calories	153
Fat	.5g
Carbohydrate	37g
Protein	1.7g
Potassium	498mg
Vitamin C	51mg
Fiber	3g

MELON
SMOOTHIES

Melons in season make some of the best smoothies on earth! A buying club near us carries bags of mixed fruit containing cantaloupe, honeydew, peaches, pineapple, and red grapes. This mixture is perfect for us during the winter, because we can pick out the kind of fruit we want to use on any given day. On other days, we just scoop out whatever comes first and make "mystery smoothies."

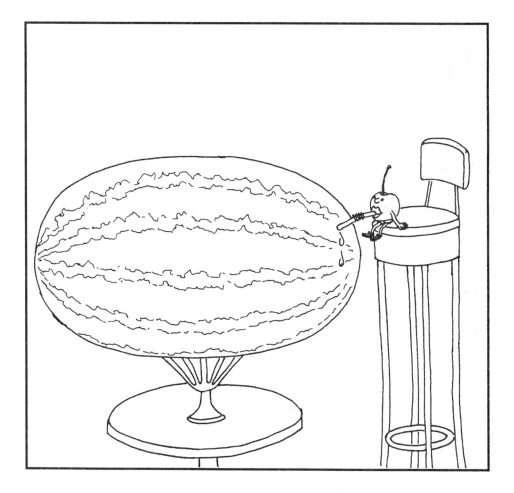

WATERMELON PEACH

1/4 c. rice milk
1/2 c. apple juice concentrate
1/2 c. applesauce
1/2 t. vanilla
4 c. watermelon chunks
1 c. frozen diced peaches

 Place rice milk (or your choice of any other milk or non-dairy substitute) and all remaining ingredients in blender in order given. (If adding protein powder, add first and blend with liquid.)

 Add one or two of the following per serving (opt.):
1/2 T. rice protein powder
1 1/2 t. flaxseed oil
1/4 t. acidophilus powder
1/8 t. vitamin C powder

 Blend until smooth and creamy. For thickest smoothies, keep blending time to a minimum.

Makes 3 cups. Serves 2. Serving Size 12 oz.

Calories	302
Fat	1g
Carbohydrate	73.5g
Protein	3.6g
Potassium	1498mg
Vitamin C	212mg
Fiber	5g

WATERMELON FRUIT PUNCH

1/4 c. oat milk
1/2 c. Dole Tropical Fruit Punch concentrate
4 c. watermelon chunks
1 c. frozen diced peaches
1/2 frozen banana

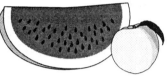

 Place oat milk (or your choice of any other milk or non-dairy substitute) and all remaining ingredients in blender in order given.

 Add one or two of the following per serving (opt.):
1-2 t. lecithin granules
1 1/2 t. flaxseed oil
1/4 t. acidophilus powder
1/8 t. vitamin C powder

 Blend until smooth and creamy. For thickest smoothies, keep blending time to a minimum.

Makes 3 cups. Serves 2. Serving Size 12 oz.

Calories	214
Fat	1.1g
Carbohydrate	52.5g
Protein	4.1g
Potassium	1270mg
Vitamin C	158mg
Fiber	4.9g

MELON 🍉 SMOOTHIES

WATERMELON FRAPPÉ

1/3 c. rice milk
2/3 c. Dole Tropical Fruit Punch concentrate
4 c. watermelon chunks
1 1/4 c. frozen red grapes
8 ice cubes

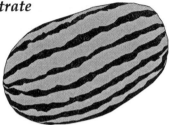

Place rice milk (or your choice of any other milk or non-dairy substitute) and all remaining ingredients in blender in order given.

Add one or two of the following per serving (opt.):
1/2 T. oat bran
1 1/2 t. flaxseed oil
1/4 t. acidophilus powder
1/8 t. vitamin C powder

Blend until smooth. For thickest smoothies, keep blending time to a minimum.

Makes 4 1/2 cups. Serves 3. Serving Size 12 oz.

Calories	153
Fat	.9g
Carbohydrate	38.3g
Protein	2.6g
Potassium	792mg
Vitamin C	106mg
Fiber	2.5g

HONEYDEW CREAM

1 c. oat milk
1/2 c. apple juice concentrate
2 1/2 c. honeydew melon (fresh or frozen)
6 ice cubes

Place oat milk (or your choice of any other milk or non-dairy substitute) and all remaining ingredients in blender in order given. (If adding protein powder, add first and blend with liquid.)

Add one or two of the following per serving (opt.):
1/2 T. rice protein powder
1 1/2 t. flaxseed oil
1/4 t. acidophilus powder
1/8 t. vitamin C powder

Blend until smooth and creamy. For thickest smoothies, keep blending time to a minimum.

Makes 4 1/2 cups. Serves 3. Serving Size 12 oz.

Calories 137
Fat 5g
Carbohydrate . . 32.4g
Protein 1.5g
Potassium 620mg
Vitamin C 105mg
Fiber 1.3g

PIÑA COLADA CREAM

1 c. oat milk
1/2 c. apple juice concentrate
1/4 t. coconut extract
1/4 t. pineapple extract
2 1/2 c. honeydew melon
10 ice cubes

 Place oat milk (or your choice of any other milk or non-dairy substitute) and all remaining ingredients in blender in order given.

 Add one or two of the following per serving (opt.):
1 T. almonds
1 1/2 t. flaxseed oil
1/4 t. acidophilus powder
1/8 t. vitamin C powder

 Blend until smooth and creamy. If desired, add optional nuts last for "crunch."

Makes 4 1/2 cups. Serves 3. Serving Size 12 oz.

Calories	137
Fat	.5g
Carbohydrate	32.4g
Protein	1.5g
Potassium	620mg
Vitamin C	105mg
Fiber	1.3g

MELON 🍉 SMOOTHIES

COUNTRY RASPBERRY CREAM

1 c. oat milk
3/4 c. Dole Country Raspberry concentrate
2 1/2 c. honeydew melon
8 ice cubes

Place oat milk (or your choice of any other milk or non-dairy substitute) and all remaining ingredients in blender in order given. (If adding protein powder, add first and blend with liquid.)

Add one or two of the following per serving (opt.):
1/2 T. rice protein powder
1 1/2 t. flaxseed oil
1/4 t. acidophilus powder
1/8 t. vitamin C powder

Blend until smooth and creamy. For thickest smoothies, keep blending time to a minimum.

Makes 4 1/2 cups. Serves 3. Serving Size 12 oz.

Calories	198
Fat	.5g
Carbohydrate	47.3g
Protein	2.5g
Potassium	643mg
Vitamin C	117mg
Fiber	1.3g

CASABA CREAM

1 c. lowfat soy milk
1/2 c. Welch's 100% White Grape juice concentrate
1/4 t. vanilla extract
2 1/2 c. casaba melon (or honeydew)
6 ice cubes

Place soy milk (or your choice of any other milk or non-dairy substitute) and all remaining ingredients in blender in order given. (If adding protein powder, add first and blend with liquid.)

Add one or two of the following per serving (opt.):
1/2 T. Natureade vegetable protein powder
1 1/2 t. flaxseed oil
1/4 t. acidophilus powder
1/8 t. vitamin C powder

Blend until smooth and creamy. For thickest smoothies, keep blending time to a minimum.

Makes 4 1/2 cups. Serves 3. Serving Size 12 oz.

Calories 175
Fat 1g
Carbohydrate .. 41.7g
Protein 2.3g
Potassium 297mg
Vitamin C 70mg
Fiber 1.5g

COCONUT CREAM

1 c. barley milk (or lowfat soy milk)
1/2 c. Welch's 100% White Grape juice concentrate
1/2 t. pure coconut extract
2 1/2 c. casaba melon (or honeydew)
8 ice cubes

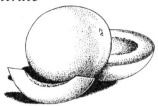

 Place barley milk (or your choice of any other milk or non-dairy substitute) and all remaining ingredients in blender in order given. (If adding protein powder or almonds, add first and blend with liquid.)

 Add one or two of the following per serving (opt.):
1/2 T. rice protein powder
1 1/2 t. flaxseed oil
1/4 t. acidophilus powder
1 T. almonds

 Blend until smooth and creamy. For thickest smoothies, keep blending time to a minimum.

Makes 4 1/2 cups. Serves 3. Serving Size 12 oz.

Calories	191
Fat	.1g
Carbohydrate	45.6g
Protein	2.6g
Potassium	372mg
Vitamin C	70mg
Fiber	2.8g

CANTALOUPE COOLER

1 c. lowfat soy or rice milk
1/2 c. apple juice concentrate
2 1/2 c. cantaloupe
6 ice cubes

 Place soy or rice milk (or your choice of any other milk or non-dairy substitute) and all remaining ingredients in blender in order given. (If adding protein powder, add first and blend with liquid.)

Add one or two of the following per serving (opt.):
1/2 T. rice protein powder
1 1/2 t. flaxseed oil
1/4 t. acidophilus powder
1/8 t. vitamin C powder

 Blend until smooth and creamy. For thickest smoothies, keep blending time to a minimum.

Makes 4 1/2 cups. Serves 3. Serving Size 12 oz.

Calories	152
Fat	3.4g
Carbohydrate	35.5g
Protein	2.2g
Potassium	609mg
Vitamin C	104mg
Fiber	1.4g

MELON DE-LITE

1 c. lowfat soy or rice milk
2/3 c. Welch's 100% White Grape juice concentrate
2 c. cantaloupe
1 1/2 c. red seedless grapes
6 ice cubes

Place soy or rice milk (or your choice of any other milk or non-dairy substitute) and all remaining ingredients in blender in order given.

Add one or two of the following per serving (opt.):
1 1/2 t. flaxseed oil
1/4 t. acidophilus powder
1 t. wheat germ
1/8 t. vitamin C powder

Blend until smooth and creamy. For thickest smoothies, keep blending time to a minimum.

Makes 6 cups. Serves 4. Serving Size 12 oz.

Calories	199
Fat	.5g
Carbohydrate	49g
Protein	1.8g
Potassium	367mg
Vitamin C	84mg
Fiber	1.6g

MELON 🍉 SMOOTHIES

HONEYDEW SPECIAL

1 c. almond milk
1/2 c. Welch's 100% White Grape juice concentrate
3 T. Better Than Milk tofu powder
1/2 t. acidophilus powder
1/4 t. vanilla extract
2 1/2 c. honeydew melon
6 ice cubes

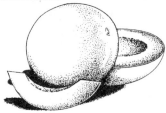

 Place almond milk (or your choice of any other milk or non-dairy substitute) and protein powder in blender. Blend until smooth. Add remaining ingredients.

 Add one or two of the following per serving (opt.):
1 1/2 t. flaxseed oil
1/8 t. vitamin C powder

 Blend until smooth and creamy. For thickest smoothies, keep blending time to a minimum.

Makes 4 1/2 cups. Serves 3. Serving Size 12 oz.

Calories	185
Fat	1.8g
Carbohydrate	41.7g
Protein	2.3g
Potassium	297mg
Vitamin C	70mg
Fiber	1.5g

MIXED FRUIT SMOOTHIES

It's hard for me to make a smoothie using only one type of fruit. I'd rather throw in a little of this and a little of that and see what happens. I love a good mystery, so I tend to make a lot of mysterious drinks!

These recipes are perfect for those of you who like to experiment. If you don't have the kind of fruit called for, use another one! I've never ruined a smoothie yet by making substitutions, so roll up your sleeves and start those creative juices flowing!

GONE PLUM BANANAS

1/2 c. barley milk
1/2 c. apple juice concentrate
3 ripe plums
1 frozen banana
6 ice cubes

Place barley milk (or your choice of any other milk or non-dairy substitute) and all remaining ingredients in blender in order given. (If adding protein powder, add first and blend with liquid.)

Add one or two of the following per serving (opt.):
1/2 T. rice protein powder
1 1/2 t. flaxseed oil
1/4 t. acidophilus powder
1/8 t. vitamin C powder

Blend until smooth and creamy. For thickest smoothies, keep blending time to a minimum.

Makes 3 cups. Serves 2. Serving Size 12 oz.

Calories 257
Fat 9g
Carbohydrate .. 61.7g
Protein 2.4g
Potassium 717mg
Vitamin C 85mg
Fiber 4.1g

GRAPE GRAPE SLUSH
by Kimm Bingham

1/3 c. Welch's 100% Grape Juice concentrate
1 c. frozen red grapes
1/3 c. nut milk
2/3 c. water
6 ice cubes

 Place nut milk (or your choice of any other milk or non-dairy substitute) and all remaining ingredients in blender in order given. (If adding protein powder, add first and blend with liquid.)

 Add one or two of the following per serving (opt.):
1/2 T. rice protein powder
1 1/2 t. flaxseed oil
1/2 T. oat bran
1/8 t. vitamin C powder

 Blend until smooth and creamy. For thickest smoothies, keep blending time to a minimum.

Makes 3 cups. Serves 2. Serving Size 12 oz.

Calories	176
Fat	.8g
Carbohydrate	42.9g
Protein	.8g
Potassium	159mg
Vitamin C	51mg
Fiber	1g

PEACH PERFECTION

by Kimm Bingham

1/3 c. Welch's 100% White Grape Peach concentrate
1/2 c. water
1/2 c. barley milk
1 c. frozen peaches, cubed
1 frozen banana
4 ice cubes

 Place barley milk (or your choice of any other milk or non-dairy substitute) and all remaining ingredients in blender in order given. (If adding protein powder, add first and blend with liquid.)

 Add one or two of the following per serving (opt.):
1/2 T. rice protein powder
1 T. chopped dates
1/4 t. acidophilus powder
1/8 t. vitamin C powder

 Blend until smooth and creamy. For thickest smoothies, keep blending time to a minimum.

Makes 3 cups. Serves 2. Serving Size 12 oz.

Calories	219
Fat	.4g
Carbohydrate	54g
Protein	2.2g
Potassium	419mg
Vitamin C	4.3g

PURPLE PEACH

by Kimm Bingham

1/3 c. Welch's 100% Grape Juice Concentrate
1/2 c. water
1/3 c. nut milk
1 c. frozen peaches, cubed
1 frozen banana
4 ice cubes

 Place nut milk (or your choice of any other milk or non-dairy substitute) and all remaining ingredients in blender in order given. (If adding protein powder, add first and blend with liquid.)

 Add one or two of the following per serving (opt.):
1/2 T. rice protein powder
1/2 T. oat bran
1/4 t. acidophilus powder
1/8 t. vitamin C powder

 Blend until smooth and creamy. For thickest smoothies, keep blending time to a minimum.

Makes 3 cups. Serves 2. Serving Size 12 oz.

Calories	213
Fat	.8g
Carbohydrate	51.4g
Protein	1.5g
Potassium	394mg
Vitamin C	58mg
Fiber	3.1g

PEACHY PINEAPPLE DELIGHT

1/2 c. water
1/2 c. barley milk
1/3 c. Welch's 100% White Grape Peach concentrate
1 1/2 c. frozen peaches, cubed
1 c. frozen pineapple chunks
1/2 t. vanilla

 Place barley milk (or your choice of any other milk or non-dairy substitute) and all remaining ingredients in blender in order given. (If adding protein powder, add first and blend with liquid.)

 Add one or two of the following per serving (opt.):
1/2 T. rice protein powder
1 1/2 t. flaxseed oil
1/4 t. acidophilus powder
1/8 t. vitamin C powder

 Blend until smooth and creamy. For thickest smoothies, keep blending time to a minimum.

Makes 4 1/2 cups. Serves 3. Serving Size 12 oz.

Calories	150
Fat	.2g
Carbohydrate	37.2g
Protein	1.6g
Potassium	289mg
Vitamin C	43mg
Fiber	3.1g

CREAMY PURPLE COW

1 c. water
1 c. rice milk
1/2 c. Welch's 100% Grape Juice concentrate
2 c. frozen red or purple grapes
2 frozen bananas
1 t. vanilla

 Place rice milk (or your choice of any other milk or non-dairy substitute) and all remaining ingredients in blender in order given. (If adding protein powder, add first and blend with liquid.)

 Add one or two of the following per serving (opt.):
1/2 T. rice protein powder
1 1/2 t. flaxseed oil
1/4 t. acidophilus powder
1 T. almonds

 Blend until smooth and creamy. If desired, add optional nuts last for "crunch."

Makes 6 cups. Serves 4. Serving Size 12 oz.

Calories 113
Fat 1g
Carbohydrate . . 27.9g
Protein 1.2g
Potassium 217mg
Vitamin C 33mg
Fiber 2.3g

MIXED FRUIT 🍎🍐 **SMOOTHIES** *Page 93*

PEACHY COOL-ER

1/2 c. Welch's 100% White Grape Peach concentrate
1 c. barley milk or plain yogurt
2 1/2 c. frozen peaches, cubed

 Place barley milk (or your choice of any other milk or non-dairy substitute) and all remaining ingredients in blender in order given. (If adding protein powder, add first and blend with liquid.)

 Add one or two of the following per serving (opt.):
1/2 T. rice protein powder
1 1/2 t. flaxseed oil
1/4 t. acidophilus powder
1/8 t. vitamin C powder

 Blend until smooth and creamy. For thickest smoothies, keep blending time to a minimum.

Makes 4 1/2 cups. Serves 3. Serving Size 12 oz.

Calories	202
Fat	.1g
Carbohydrate	49.3g
Protein	2.3g
Potassium	315mg
Vitamin C	57mg
Fiber	4.5g

PEACH DE-LITE

1/2 c. water
1 c. barley milk
1/2 c. Welch's 100% White Grape Peach concentrate
1 1/4 c. frozen cantaloupe
1 1/2 c. frozen peaches
1 frozen banana

 Place barley milk (or your choice of any other milk or non-dairy substitute) and all remaining ingredients in blender in order given. (If adding protein powder, add first and blend with liquid.)

 Add one or two of the following per serving (opt.):
1/2 T. rice protein powder
1 T. sunflower seeds
1/4 t. acidophilus powder
1/8 t. vitamin C powder

 Blend until smooth and creamy. If desired, add optional sunflower (raw or toasted) seeds last for "crunch."

Makes 4 1/2 cups. Serves 3. Serving Size 12 oz.

Calories	236
Fat	.5g
Carbohydrate	57.5g
Protein	2.9g
Potassium	559mg
Vitamin C	84mg
Fiber	4.8g

CREAMY BANANA BERRY

1/2 c. oat milk
1/2 c. Dole Pineapple Orange Strawberry concentrate
3 T. tofu powder or protein powder
1/4 c. fresh or frozen avocado
1 1/2 c. frozen strawberries
1 frozen banana
3-6 ice cubes, depending on thickness desired

 Place oat milk (or your choice of any other milk or non-dairy substitute) and all remaining ingredients in blender in order given.

 Add one or two of the following per serving (opt.):
1 1/2 t. flaxseed oil
1/4 t. acidophilus powder
1/8 t. vitamin C powder

 Blend until smooth and creamy. For thickest smoothies, keep blending time to a minimum.

Makes 4 1/2 cups. Serves 3. Serving Size 12 oz.

Calories	219
Fat	5.9g
Carbohydrate	41.6g
Protein	2.9g
Potassium	687mg
Vitamin C	87mg
Fiber	3.8g

CRANAPPLE

1/2 c. water
1/2 c. oat milk
1/2 c. Welch's 100% White Grape Cranberry concentrate
1/2 c. applesauce
4-8 large ice cubes, depending on thickness desired

Place oat milk (or your choice of any other milk or non-dairy substitute) and all remaining ingredients in blender in order given. (If adding protein powder, add first and blend with liquid.)

Add one or two of the following per serving (opt.):
1/2 T. rice protein powder
1 t. brewer's yeast
1/4 t. acidophilus powder
1/8 t. vitamin C powder

Blend until smooth and creamy. For thickest smoothies, keep blending time to a minimum.

Makes 3 cups. Serves 2. Serving Size 12 oz.

Calories 192
Fat 1g
Carbohydrate .. 47g
Protein 3g
Potassium 54mg
Vitamin C 73mg
Fiber 9g

CRANBERRY SLUSH

1/4 c. water
1/2 c. barley milk
1/2 c. Welch's 100% White Grape Cranberry concentrate
1 frozen banana
6 lg. ice cubes

Place barley milk (or your choice of any other milk or non-dairy substitute) and all remaining ingredients in blender in order given. (If adding protein powder, add first and blend with liquid.)

Add one or two of the following per serving (opt.):
1/2 T. rice protein powder
1/8 c. aloe vera juice
1/4 t. acidophilus powder
1/8 t. vitamin C powder

Blend until smooth and creamy. For thickest smoothies, keep blending time to a minimum.

Makes 3 cups. Serves 2. Serving Size 12 oz.

Calories	242
Fat	.3g
Carbohydrate	58.7g
Protein	1.6g
Potassium	251mg
Vitamin C	76mg
Fiber	2.6g

CRANANNA

1/2 c. water
1/2 c. oat milk
3/4 c. Welch's 100% White Grape Cranberry concentrate
1/2 t. vanilla
1/2 c. lite tofu
2 large peaches, frozen
1 banana, fresh or frozen
8 lg. ice cubes

Place oat milk (or your choice of any other milk or non-dairy substitute) and all remaining ingredients in blender in order given.

Add one or two of the following per serving (opt.):
1 1/2 t. flaxseed oil
1/4 t. acidophilus powder
1/8 t. vitamin C powder

Blend until smooth and creamy. For thickest smoothies, keep blending time to a minimum.

Makes 6 cups. Serves 4. Serving Size 12 oz.

Calories	177
Fat	.5g
Carbohydrate	41.5g
Protein	2.3g
Potassium	203mg
Vitamin C	59mg
Fiber	1.6g

CREAMY PEACH

1/2 c. water
1/2 c. oat milk
3/4 c. apple juice concentrate
1/2 t. vanilla
1" slice lite tofu
1 1/2 c. frozen peaches, cubed
1 frozen banana

 Place oat milk (or your choice of any other milk or non-dairy substitute) and all remaining ingredients in blender in order given.

 Add one or two of the following per serving (opt.):
1 1/2 t. flaxseed oil
1/4 t. acidophilus powder
1 T. almonds
1/8 t. vitamin C powder

 Blend until smooth and creamy. If desired, add optional nuts last for "crunch."

Makes 4 1/2 cups. Serves 3. Serving Size 12 oz.

Calories 206
Fat 7g
Carbohydrate . . 48.5g
Protein 2.8g
Potassium 620mg
Vitamin C 81mg
Fiber 2.7g

POLKA DOT PEACH

(This drink gets its name from the pieces of grape skins that remain after blending.)

1/2 c. water
1/2 c. oat milk
3/4 c. apple juice concentrate
1/2 t. vanilla
1" slice lite tofu
1 1/2 c. frozen peaches, cubed

1 c. frozen red seedless grapes
1 frozen banana

 Place oat milk (or your choice of any other milk or non-dairy substitute) and all remaining ingredients in blender in order given.

 Add one or two of the following per serving (opt.):
1 1/2 t. flaxseed oil
1/4 t. acidophilus powder
1/8 t. vitamin C powder

 Blend until smooth and creamy. For thickest smoothies, keep blending time to a minimum.

Makes 4 1/2 cups. Serves 3. Serving Size 12 oz.

Calories	236
Fat	.8g
Carbohydrate	56.9g
Protein	3g
Potassium	720mg
Vitamin C	82mg
Fiber	3.3g

APPLE APRICOT

1 3/4 c. Knudsen Apple-Apricot juice
1/4 c. oat milk
2 frozen bananas
1/4" slice firm lite tofu

 Place oat milk (or your choice of any other milk or non-dairy substitute) and all remaining ingredients in blender in order given.

 Add one or two of the following per serving (opt.):
1 1/2 t. flaxseed oil
1/4 t. acidophilus powder
1/8 t. vitamin C powder

 Blend until smooth and creamy. For thickest smoothies, keep blending time to a minimum.

Makes 3 cups. Serves 2. Serving Size 12 oz.

```
Calories  . . . . . . . 224
Fat . . . . . . . . . . . . .8g
Carbohydrate  . . 55.4g
Protein  . . . . . . . . 2g
Potassium  . . . . . 676mg
Vitamin C  . . . . . 46mg
Fiber  . . . . . . . . . . 2.8g
```

WHITE GRAPRICOT

2 1/4 c. Knudsen Apple-Apricot juice
1/4 c. oat milk
1/4 c. Welch's 100% White Grape juice concentrate
1/4" slice firm tofu
1 frozen banana

 Place oat milk (or your choice of any other milk or non-dairy substitute) and all remaining ingredients in blender in order given.

 Add one or two of the following per serving (opt.):
1 1/2 t. flaxseed oil
1/4 t. acidophilus powder
1/8 t. vitamin C powder

 Blend until smooth and creamy. For thickest smoothies, keep blending time to a minimum.

Makes 3 cups. Serves 2. Serving Size 12 oz.

Calories	284
Fat	.5g
Carbohydrate	69.9g
Protein	1.4g
Potassium	506mg
Vitamin C	86mg
Fiber	1.5g

CREAMY PEAR COOLER

1 c. barley milk
1/2 c. apple juice concentrate
3 ripe pears
6 ice cubes

 Place barley milk (or your choice of any other milk or non-dairy substitute) and all remaining ingredients in blender in order given. (If adding protein powder, add first and blend with liquid.)

 Add one or two of the following per serving (opt.):
1/2 T. rice protein powder
1 1/2 t. flaxseed oil
1/4 t. acidophilus powder
1/8 t. vitamin C powder

 Blend until smooth and creamy. For thickest smoothies, keep blending time to a minimum.

Makes 4 1/2 cups. Serves 3. Serving Size 12 oz.

Calories	219
Fat	.7g
Carbohydrate	53.3g
Protein	2g
Potassium	439mg
Vitamin C	54mg
Fiber	5.6g

PEAR FOOLER

This drink fooled my daughter who doesn't like pears. She loved it!

1 c. barley milk
1/2 c. Welch's 100% White Grape Juice concentrate
1/4" slice firm tofu
3 ripe pears
6 ice cubes

 Place barley milk (or your choice of any other milk or non-dairy substitute) and all remaining ingredients in blender in order given.

 Add one or two of the following per serving (opt.):
1 1/2 t. flaxseed oil
1/4 t. acidophilus powder
1 T. sunflower seeds
1/8 t. vitamin C powder

 Blend until smooth and creamy. For thickest smoothies, keep blending time to a minimum.

Makes 4 1/2 cups. Serves 3. Serving Size 12 oz.

Calories	254
Fat	.7g
Carbohydrate	62g
Protein	2.4g
Potassium	242mg
Vitamin C	54mg
Fiber	5.6g

SWEET RASPBERRY CREAM

1/2 c. Welch's 100% White Grape Raspberry juice concentrate
3/4 c. low fat soy milk
1 t. vanilla extract
2 ripe pears
1 frozen banana
6 ice cubes

 Place soy milk (or your choice of any other milk or non-dairy substitute) and all remaining ingredients in blender in order given. (If adding protein powder, add first and blend with liquid.)

 Add one or two of the following per serving (opt.):
1/2 T. rice protein powder
1 1/2 t. flaxseed oil
1/4 t. acidophilus powder
1/2 T. oat bran

 Blend until smooth and creamy. For thickest smoothies, keep blending time to a minimum.

Makes 4 1/2 cups. Serves 3. Serving Size 12 oz.

Calories	220
Fat	.6g
Carbohydrate	53.4g
Protein	1.6g
Potassium	289mg
Vitamin C	55mg
Fiber	3.8g

℞ SMOOTHIES

For those who like to do a little doctorin'

I grew up in a family that practiced a lot of preventive health measures, from sweat baths to green drinks, throat wraps to herbal tonics. We still do all that, but these Rx Smoothies are a very pleasurable way to get some extra nutrients, cool off a fever, or soothe a sore throat.

Many common ailments are treated with the same nutrients, usually vitamins A, C, E, Beta Carotene, Zinc and Acidophilus. Why? Because these are the best nutrients for boosting the body's immune system so it can do its best to heal quickly. It is best to consume lots of liquids: water, fresh fruit and vegetable juices. Protein from vegetable sources is easier for the body to process, so stay away from meats when you're trying to rebuild health. Eat as many raw foods as possible (whole or juiced). Smoothies to the rescue!

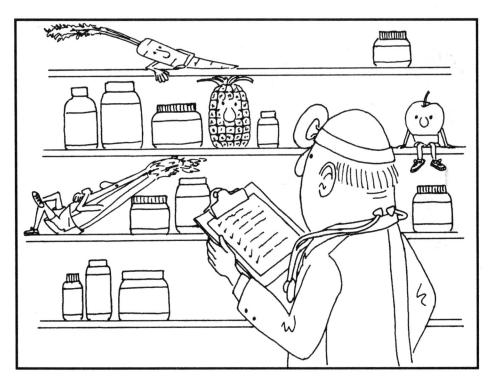

VITAMIN C ISLAND SPECIAL

Wish you could head for a tropical island at the first sign of a cold? This drink will make you think you're on your way! It's filled with nutrients that can help boost your immune system and speed your recovery. When you're "under the weather" and don't FEEL like preparing a nutritious meal, make this Rx smoothie!

3 T. Natureade Vegetable Protein Powder
1 c. carrot juice   **1 T. flaxseed oil**
2 lg. frozen bananas   **1/2 t. vitamin C powder**
1 large frozen peach   **1/2 t. acidophilus powder**
1/2 c. Dole Pineapple Orange Banana concentrate

Place all ingredients in blender in order given.

Blend protein powder and carrot juice until creamy. Add remaining ingredients and blend until smooth.

Makes 3 cups. Serves 2. Serving Size 12 oz.

Doctorin' Tips:
The following have been helpful in fighting cold viruses and boosting the immune system: vitamin C (1,000 to 2,000 mg. daily, in divided doses), acidophilus (to replace "friendly" bacteria), and 5-30 drops of Nutribiotic GSE (Grapefruit Seed Extract) to destroy bacteria and viruses. For more information on GSE, or to order, call 1-888-232-6706.

Cal. 363, Fat 8 g, Carb. 62.6g, Pro. 15g, Pot. 882mg, Vit. C 1239mg, Fib. 4.1g

IMMUNE SYSTEM BOOSTER

If you've got a cold, or the flu, your immune system needs a boost! Stay away from sugars (even artificial ones), and add as many immune-building nutrients as possible to your smoothies.

1 1/2 c. carrot juice (or water)   2 T. flaxseed oil
2 lg. frozen bananas   1/2 t. vitamin C crystals
1 c. frozen peach chunks   1 t. acidophilus powder
1 c. frozen pineapple chunks
1/4 c. Dole Pineapple Orange Banana concentrate

Place all ingredients in blender in order given.

Blend protein powder and carrot juice until creamy. Add remaining ingredients and blend until smooth.

Makes 4 1/2 cups. Serves 3. Serving Size 12 oz.

Doctorin' Tips:
If you're really "down," divide this drink into three glasses and drink throughout the day, or freeze in 5-oz. paper cups, inserting a stick or a spoon for a handle, and eat as a popsicle.

Be sure and concentrate on eating foods high in Vitamins A, C, E, Beta-Carotene, Zinc (all the dark-colored ones like spinach, broccoli, winter squashes, carrots, etc.).

Cal.279, Fat 10.7 g, Carb. 48.3g, Pro. 2.5g, Pot. 906mg, Vit. C 818mg, Fib. 5.5g

FATIGUE FIGHTER

Fatigue is a symptom that something is wrong in the body. If it is not related to a lack of sleep, then you need to look at it as an early symptom of a health problem.

1/2 c. almond milk
1 T. rice protein powder
1/2 t. vitamin C powder
1" slice lite tofu
1/2 c. Welch's 100% White Grape
   Peach concentrate

3/4 c. frozen peaches
4 ice cubes
2 T. toasted sunflower seeds

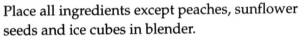

1 Place all ingredients except peaches, sunflower seeds and ice cubes in blender.

2 Blend until creamy. Add frozen peaches and ice and blend just until smooth. Add sunflower seeds and blend for about 5 seconds.

Makes 3 cups. Serves 2. Serving Size 12 oz.

3 **Doctorin' Tips:**

A diet high in fats, refined carbohydrates (white sugar, white flour, most pasta) and caffeine not only fails to supply the body with energy, it depletes the body of essential B-vitamins - a sort of "doubly whammy" on the body's energy. The solution: lots of fresh fruits and veggies (especially dark green, leafy veggies), whole grains, beans, raw seeds and raw nuts. In addition, take plenty of vitamin C and amino acids, get plenty of exercise, adequate rest, and plan for some time during each day when you can take a mental "time out" to give your brain a break and relax tense muscles.

Cal. 193, Fat 6.3 g, Carb. 26.1g, Pro. 11.5g, Pot. 392mg, Vit. C1176mg, Fib. 2.7g

℞ SMOOTHIES

FEVER BUSTER

Rather than reach for an aspirin, reach for a Smoothie Pop!

3/4 c. barley milk
1/2 t. vitamin C powder
1/4 c. Knudsen's Black Cherry Juice
3/4 c. apple juice concentrate
1 frozen banana

Place all ingredients in blender in order given.

Blend until smooth. Pour into 3-oz. paper cups, insert a stick for a handle and freeze until firm. Smoothie will be sweeter than normal for use as smoothie pops.

Makes 3 cups. Serves 2. Serving Size 12 oz.

Doctorin' Tips:
A fever is the body's immune system's way of destroying harmful microbes. It is best to let the fever run its course, without administering medications, unless the body temperature rises above 102°F in adults or 103°F in children. These frosty fruit smoothie pops will help temporarily ease the discomfort and provide much-needed nourishment to help boost the immune system. Be sure to drink plenty of water and fresh juices.

Cal. 100, Fat .1 g, Carb. 24g, Pro. .8g, Pot. 247mg, Vit. C 426mg, Fib. 1.1g

FLU BUG BOMBER

7 fruit juices and vital nutrients to help you take charge of your health.

1 c. Knudsen's Vita Juice
1/2 banana
2 t. rice protein powder
1/2 ripe pear
1/2 t. vitamin C powder
1/2 t. acidophilus powder
15 drops Nutribiotic GSE liquid concentrate
6 ice cubes
1/2 c. Dole Pineapple Orange Banana concentrate

Place all but ice and fruit juice concentrate in blender in order given.

Blend long enough to get the protein powder smooooth, then add ice cubes and concentrate and blend again.

Makes 3 cups. Serves 2. Serving Size 12 oz.

Doctorin' Tips:

When you have the flu, you usually don't FEEL like eating, but the body still needs nutrients like Vitamins A, C, E, and Zinc. This smoothie will help ease a dry throat and cough, cool off a fever, give you nutrients to fight fatigue, and help you toward a speedy recovery.

(Influenza is highly contagious, so give your body the break it needs and get plenty of rest and plenty of fluids, including fruit smoothies!) GSE (up to 30 drops daily) "bombs" the flu in 1-2 days for my family!!

Cal. 257, Fat .3 g, Carb. 58.4g, Pro. 6.4g, Pot. 618mg, Vit. C 1260mg, Fib. 1.7g

SORE THROAT SOOTHER

At the first sign of a sore throat, a good boost to the immune system can often help the body fight off more serious disorders. Since most sore throats are caused by viral infections, antibiotics are ineffective. Nutrients to boost the immune system so the body can fight the viruses are easy to add to smoothies, and this frosty drink will help ease a sore or irritated throat as well as feed a weakened immune system.

1/2 c. Dole Pineapple Orange Banana concentrate
1 c. rice milk   **1 frozen banana**
1/2 t. vitamin C powder   **6 ice cubes**

Place all ingredients in blender in order given.

Blend until smooth and creamy.

Makes 3 cups. Serves 2. Serving Size 12 oz.

Doctorin' Tips:

For a SUPER sore throat, make a mixture of 1 T. honey, 1 t. lemon juice, and 1/4 t. vitamin C powder. Take 1/2 t. by mouth and swallow only a little bit at a time to allow mixture to coat and sooth the throat. (Granny's best before-bed sore throat remedy is to rub chest and throat with Mentholatum, then wrap throat with a cotton cloth soaked in very cold water. Cover with another cotton cloth, or an old tube sock. Pin into place. The cold cloth against the Mentholatum increases circulation which in turn speeds healing.)

Cal. 210, Fat .3 g, Carb. 50.8g, Pro. 2.1g, Pot. 571mg, Vit. C 1231mg, Fib. 1.4g

CRANBERRY CRUSH

For bladder and kidney problems, drink 1 quart of unsweetened cranberry juice per day and at least 2 quarts of water.

1 c. Knudsen's Just Cranberry juice
2 T. celery juice-blend with
cranberry juice and water,
then strain out
1/4 c. apple juice concentrate

1/2 t. acidophilus powder
1 frozen banana
1/2 t. vitamin C powder
10 large ice cubes

Place all ingredients in blender in order given.

Blend until smooth.

Makes 3 cups. Serves 2. Serving Size 12 oz.

Doctorin' Tips:

Celery, parsley and watermelon are natural diuretics and cleansers. Avoid citrus fruits. Take 1/4 t. acidophilus powder three times per day.

Cal. 186, Fat .4 g, Carb. 46.4g, Pro. .7g, Pot. 451mg, Vit. C 86mg, Fib. 1.6g

R₂ SMOOTHIES

CANDIDA CRUSHER

Acidophilus powder or capsules aids in reestablishing normal intestinal flora to fight candida. For those who cannot tolerate dairy products of any kind, buy dairy-free acidophilus powder.

3/4 c. V-8 juice
3/4 c. fresh carrot juice
1/4 c. celery juice- blend with
  cranberry juice and water,
  then strain out
2 T. beet juice

1 vegetable bouillon cube
1/2 t. vitamin C powder
1/2 t. acidophilus powder
1 frozen banana
12 ice cubes

Place all ingredients in blender in order given.

Blend until smooth.

Makes 3 cups. Serves 2. Serving Size 12 oz.

Doctorin' Tips:

Avoid all dairy products, refined carbohydrates and sugars, including fruits (except an occasional banana) and fruit juices and sweeteners of any kind until the infection is healed, as fungus multiplies in a sugary environment. Eat lots of veggies, brown rice and other whole grains. Soured milk products contain microorganisms (Lactobacillus and L. bifidus) that help reestablish normal intestinal flora. Aloe vera is known to aid in yeast infections as well as many internal and external problems.

Cal. 53, Fat .3 g, Carb. 11.7g, Pro. 1.5g, Pot. 553mg, Vit. C 612mg, Fib. 2.4g

℞ SMOOTHIES

STRESS BUSTER

Stress, which results from both physical and psychological things, is an unavoidable part of life. For some, starting a new job, overwork, lack of sleep, extremes in temperature, crowds, and noise are stressful. Extra calcium helps the body cope better.

1/2 c. Dole Pineapple Orange concentrate
1 c. soy milk   **1 T. Barlean's flaxseed oil**
1 c. frozen peaches   **1/4 t. vitamin C powder**
1/2 t. vanilla extract
1 t. powdered calcium

Place all ingredients in blender in order given.

Blend until smooth.

Makes 2 cups. Serves 1. Serving Size 16 oz.

Doctorin' Tips:
Stress suppresses the immune system and causes the body to be depleted of valuable nutrients, especially calcium, magnesium, B complex and vitamin C. Avoid processed foods, including artificial sweeteners, soft drinks, white flour products, and dairy products. Eat a diet of mostly raw foods, including lots of fresh fruits and vegetables. Exercise regularly. Learn biofeedback to relax muscles and breathe deeply.

Cal. 513, Fat 14.9 g, Carb. 92.1g, Pro. 6.1g, Pot. 1026mg, Vit. C 1297mg, Fib. 5.5g

℞ SMOOTHIES

SUPERCHARGED SMOOTHIES

"Charged" with super nutritious ingredients

These smoothies are great for those who want to make a meal of a smoothie, and for people who need to pack in as much nutrition as possible during the day.

*They contain added ingredients like **flaxseed oil** (rich in omega-3 essential fatty acids to help with arthritis, eczema, and in lowering cholesterol and triglyceride levels), **acidophilus** (the "friendly" bacteria that helps in the digestion of proteins, helps reduce cholesterol, aids digestion and is antifungal to help fight candida), **vitamin C** (antioxidant, required for tissue growth and repair, helps wounds and bruises heal faster, boost immune system to fight colds, flu, etc.), **brewer's yeast** (rich in B vitamins, amino acids and minerals for a quick, but long-lasting energy boost), **aloe vera juice** (skin healer, infections, relieves constipation and symptoms of arthritis), **protein powder** (balanced vegetable protein, usually from rice or soybeans, for growth and development, the manufacture of hormones, antibodies, enzymes and tissues), **liquid chlorophyll** (blood cleanser and detoxifier and good source of minerals and enzymes, and **tofu** (a complete protein that is better utilized by the body than meat).*

VITA CAROTENE SPECIAL

2 T. soy protein powder
3/4 c. Knudsen Papaya Juice
1/2 c. apple juice concentrate
1/2 c. fresh carrot juice
1/4 c. canned pumpkin, unsweetened
1/2 t. vanilla extract

1/4 t. vitamin C powder
1/2 t. acidophilus powder
1 frozen banana
6 ice cubes

Place all ingredients in blender in order given.

Add one or two of the following per serving (opt.):
1 1/2 t. flaxseed oil
1 t. lecithin granules

Blend until smooth and creamy. For thickest smoothies, keep blending time to a minimum.

Makes 4 1/2 cups. Serves 3. Serving Size 12 oz.

Calories 208
Fat 5g
Carbohydrate . . 42.5g
Protein 9g
Potassium 515mg
Vitamin C 443mg
Fiber 2.4g

VITA JUICY

2 -3 T. soy protein powder
1/4 c. low fat soy milk
1/2 c. apple juice concentrate
1/2 c. Knudsen Vita Juice
1/2 t. vanilla extract

1/4 t. vitamin C powder
1/2 t. acidophilus powder
1 frozen banana (opt.)
12 ice cubes

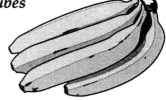

 Place first four ingredients in blender.

 Add one or two of the following per serving (opt.):
1 1/2 t. flaxseed oil
1/2 T. oat bran

 Blend until protein powder is well dissolved. Add remaining ingredients and blend until smooth.

Makes 3 cups. Serves 2. Serving Size 12 oz.

Calories 243
Fat 6g
Carbohydrate . . 51.2g
Protein 8.6g
Potassium 584mg
Vitamin C 674mg
Fiber 1.5g

SUPERCHARGED SMOOTHIES

HI-PRO JUICE-PLUS

2 T. soy protein powder
1/4 c. low fat soy milk
1/2 c. apple juice concentrate
1/2 c. Knudsen Vita Juice
2 T. George's Always Active Aloe Juice
1/2 t. vanilla extract
1/2 t. flax seed oil

1 frozen banana
12 ice cubes

 Blend protein powder until smooth with all but banana and ice. (Soy milk can be substituted with your choice of any other milk or non-dairy substitute.)

 Add one or two of the following per serving (opt.):
1/4 t. acidophilus powder
1/8 t. vitamin C powder

 Blend until smooth and creamy. For thickest smoothies, keep blending time to a minimum.

Makes 3 cups. Serves 2. Serving Size 12 oz.

Calories	250
Fat	1.8g
Carbohydrate	52.9g
Protein	6.4g
Potassium	635mg
Vitamin C	92mg
Fiber	1.6g

BERRY NUTRITIOUS

Contains added acidophilus and vitamin C for better daily digestion and resistance. Increased amounts are known to be helpful for colds and flu.

1/2 c. soy milk
1/2" slice firm tofu
4 fresh or frozen strawberries
1/4 c. Dole Country Raspberry concentrate
1/2 t. powdered vitamin C
1/2 t. acidophilus powder

3 ripe pears, cored
6 ice cubes

 Place soy milk (or your choice of any other milk or non-dairy substitute) and all remaining ingredients in blender in order given.

 Add one or two of the following per serving (opt.):
1 1/2 t. flaxseed oil
2 t. toasted sunflower seeds

 Blend until smooth and creamy. For thickest smoothies, keep blending time to a minimum.

Makes 4 1/2 cups. Serves 3. Serving Size 12 oz.

Calories	209
Fat	1.6g
Carbohydrate	50.5g
Protein	3g
Potassium	611mg
Vitamin C	917mg
Fiber	8.6g

EYE OPENER

1/2 c. low fat soy milk
1/2 c. Knudsen's Apricot Juice
1/4 c. orange juice concentrate
1/4 c. apple juice concentrate
1/4 c. George's Always Active Aloe Juice
1/4 t. powdered vitamin C
1/2 t. vanilla extract
1/4 c. lite tofu
12 ice cubes

 Place soy milk (or your choice of any other milk or non-dairy substitute) and all remaining ingredients in blender in order given.

 Add one or two of the following per serving (opt.):
1 1/2 t. flaxseed oil
1/4 t. acidophilus powder

 Blend until smooth and creamy. For thickest smoothies, keep blending time to a minimum.

Makes 3 cups. Serves 2. Serving Size 12 oz.

Calories	191
Fat	.5g
Carbohydrate	43.1g
Protein	3.7g
Potassium	532mg
Vitamin C	638mg
Fiber	.6g

HI-PRO MAPLE CREAM

This is a big meal for 2 in a small package! It's a great "Power Lunch"

1/2 c. barley milk
1/3 c. apple juice concentrate
3 T. rice protein powder
3 T. pure maple syrup
1/4 t. vanilla extract
1 large frozen banana

Place barley milk (or your choice of any other milk or non-dairy substitute), apple juice concentrate and protein powder in blender and process until smooth. Add remaining ingredients.

Add one or two of the following per serving (opt.):
1 1/2 t. flaxseed oil
1/4 t. acidophilus powder
1/8 t. vitamin C powder
1 T. toasted sunflower seeds or almonds

Blend until smooth and creamy. If adding seeds or nuts, add first to make them creamy, or just before end of blending time to keep them chunky.

Makes 3 cups. Serves 2. Serving Size 12 oz.

Calories 325
Fat 4g
Carbohydrate .. 61.9g
Protein 19.6g
Potassium 449mg
Vitamin C 52.mg
Fiber 2.9g

HI-PRO DOUBLE BLUEBERRY

1 c. rice milk
2/3 c. apple juice concentrate
1/4 c. 100% blueberry fruit spread
2-4 T. rice protein powder
1 T. flaxseed oil
1/2 t. vanilla
1 1/2 c. frozen blueberries
16 ice cubes

Place rice milk (or your choice of any other milk or non-dairy substitute) and protein powder in blender and process until smooth. Add remaining ingredients.

Add one or two of the following per serving (opt.):
1/4 t. acidophilus powder
1/8 t. vitamin C powder

Blend until smooth and creamy. For thickest smoothies, keep blending time to a minimum.

Makes 4 1/2 cups. Serves 3. Serving Size 12 oz.

Calories	304
Fat	2.1g
Carbohydrate	54.7g
Protein	16.8g
Potassium	327mg
Vitamin C	73mg
Fiber	2.3g

POWER-PACKED RASPBERRY

*Surprisingly Delicious! - great way to start the day -
breakfast in a glass..meal in a glass..snack in a glass, etc.*

1/2 c. rice milk
1 t. brewer's yeast
2 T. rice protein powder
1/2 t. acidophilus powder
1 T. flaxseed oil
2/3 c. Welch's 100% White Grape Raspberry concentrate

1/2 t. vitamin C powder
1 t. liquid chlorophyll
2 frozen bananas
12 ice cubes

Place rice milk (or your choice of any other milk or non-dairy substitute), brewer's yeast and protein powder in blender and process until smooth. Add remaining ingredients.

Add one or two of the following per serving a few seconds before end of blending time (opt):
2 t. toasted sunflower seeds
2 t. almonds

Blend until smooth and creamy. For thickest smoothies, keep blending time to a minimum.

Makes 3 cups. Serves 2. Serving Size 12 oz.

Calories 399
Fat 3.2g
Carbohydrate . . 79.8g
Protein 13.9g
Potassium 478mg
Vitamin C 1292mg
Fiber 3.5g

SUPERCHARGED ⚡ **SMOOTHIES**

HEALTHY HAWAIIAN SUNRISE

1 1/4 c. rice milk
1/3 c. pineapple juice concentrate
2 t. flaxseed oil
1/2 t. vitamin C powder

1/2 t. acidophilus powder
1 large frozen banana
10 ice cubes

Place rice milk (or your choice of any other milk or non-dairy substitute) and all remaining ingredients in blender in order given. (If adding protein powder, add first and blend with liquid.)

Add one or two of the following per serving (opt.):
1/2 T. rice protein powder
1 t. sunflower seeds

Blend until smooth and creamy. For thickest smoothies, keep blending time to a minimum.

Makes 3 cups. Serves 2. Serving Size 12 oz.

Calories	183
Fat	1.5g
Carbohydrate	42.8g
Protein	1.9g
Potassium	406mg
Vitamin C	1242mg
Fiber	1.4g

FRUIT SURPRISE

This is a good standard "healthy" smoothie. By varying the type of fruit, each smoothie is an "original." Use any kind of mixed fruit. I like bananas, cantaloupe, pineapple and grapes best.

1 c. water
2 c. any kind of milk
1/2 c. pineapple, apple or 100%
 white grape juice concentrate
1/4 c. any kind of protein powder

1/2 t. acidophilus powder
2 c. frozen fruit chunks
2 t. flaxseed oil
1/2 t. vitamin C

Place water, milk, fruit juice concentrate and protein powder in blender and process until protein powder is no longer grainy. Add remaining ingredients and process until smooth.

Add one or two of the following per serving (opt.):
2 t. sunflower seeds
1 t. oat bran
1 t. wheat germ

Blend until smooth and creamy. For thickest smoothies, keep blending time to a minimum.

Makes 6 cups. Serves 4. Serving Size 12 oz.

Calories	209
Fat	.5g
Carbohydrate	39.1g
Protein	13.8g
Potassium	416mg
Vitamin C	655mg
Fiber	1.7g

THE WORKS

We decided to pull out all the stops and see how much "good stuff" we could add and still have it taste like something you'd want to try again.

1/2 c. rice milk
2 t. raw sesame tahini
2 t. brewer's yeast
2 T. rice protein powder
1/2 t. acidophilus powder
1 T. flaxseed oil
2/3 c. Welch's 100% White Grape Raspberry concentrate

1/2 t. vitamin C powder
1/3 c. George's Always
    Active Aloe Juice
2 t. liquid chlorophyll
2 frozen bananas
12 ice cubes

Place all ingredients except bananas and ice in blender in order given.

Blend until protein powder is no longer grainy. Add bananas and ice cubes and blend again until smooth.

Makes 3 cups. Serves 2. Serving Size 12 oz.

The green chlorophyll turns the color from red to grey (still "greyt" tasting), so you may want to cut back on the quantity until you get "hooked" on the flavor. This is a great drink to experiment with adding or substituting your own favorite nutrients.

Cal. 444, Fat 4.8 g, Carb. 86.2g, Pro. 15.8g, Pot. 679mg, Vit. C 1316mg, Fib. 4.2g

TROPICAL SMOOTHIES

Frosty fruit drinks with the taste of the tropics

My husband and I met while going to school in Hawaii, so tropical fruits bring back many happy memories. While some fruits may not be readily available (or affordable) year-round (except for bananas which are always in season), canned, bottled and frozen fruit juices and concentrates are. AND, they're delicious. With the addition of coconut extract (the flavor without the fat), almost any smoothie can go tropical!

Hint: When you see bananas or other fruit on sale, buy a bunch and freeze the excess for the off-season. While freezing does destroy some nutrients, a frozen fruit (purchased at an affordable price) is lots more nutritious than NO fruit at all. Frozen bananas are best stored in a regular freezer, as the air circulation in frost-free freezers will turn them brown within a few weeks.

PINEAPPLE BANANA FREEZE

Bonus: potassium, protein

1 c. water
1 1/4 c. oat milk
1 c. Dole Pineapple-Orange concentrate
12 oz. pkg. firm lite tofu
2 frozen bananas
12 ice cubes

Place oat milk (or your choice of any other milk or non-dairy substitute) and all remaining ingredients in blender in order given. (If adding protein powder, add first and blend with liquid.)

Add one or two of the following per serving (opt.):
1/2 T. rice protein powder
1 1/2 t. flaxseed oil
1/4 t. acidophilus powder
1/8 t. vitamin C powder

Blend until smooth and creamy. For thickest smoothies, keep blending time to a minimum.

Makes 4 1/2 cups. Serves 3. Serving Size 12 oz.

Calories	292
Fat	1.7g
Carbohydrate	63g
Protein	9.2g
Potassium	761mg
Vitamin C	86mg
Fiber	1.8g

MANGO PINEAPPLE FRAPPÉ

1/4 c. barley milk
1/2 c. Dole Pineapple-Orange concentrate
3/4 c. pineapple juice
1/2 c. mango pieces
1 frozen banana
6 ice cubes

 Place barley milk (or your choice of any other milk or non-dairy substitute) and all remaining ingredients in blender in order given. (If adding protein powder, add first and blend with liquid.)

 Add one or two of the following per serving (opt.):
1/2 T. rice protein powder
1 1/2 t. flaxseed oil
1/4 t. acidophilus powder
1/8 t. vitamin C powder

 Blend until smooth and creamy. For thickest smoothies, keep blending time to a minimum.

Makes 3 cups. Serves 2. Serving Size 12 oz.

Calories	401
Fat	.4g
Carbohydrate	99.4g
Protein	3.9g
Potassium	1055mg
Vitamin C	232mg
Fiber	2.7g

TROPICAL 🍍 SMOOTHIES

TROPICAL ENERGIZER

1/2 c. almond milk
1 T. rice protein powder
1/2 c. Welch's 100% White Grape Peach concentrate
1/2 t. vitamin C powder
1" slice tofu
1 frozen banana
3/4 c. frozen peaches
2 T. toasted sunflower seeds

Place almond milk and protein powder in blender and process until smooth. Add all remaining ingredients, except sunflower seeds, in order given. (Add sunflower seeds after initial blending and blend for about 5 seconds.)

Add one or two of the following per serving (opt.):
1 1/2 t. flaxseed oil
1/4 t. acidophilus powder

Blend until smooth and creamy. For thickest smoothies, keep blending time to a minimum.

Makes 3 cups. Serves 2. Serving Size 12 oz.

```
Calories  . . . . . . . 361
Fat . . . . . . . . . . . 6.3g
Carbohydrate  . . 67.5g
Protein  . . . . . . . . 11.5g
Potassium  . . . . . 392mg
Vitamin C  . . . . . 1247mg
Fiber  . . . . . . . . . . 2.7g
```

BANANA CREME

2 c. ice water
1 c. barley milk
1/2 c. Natureade Vegetable Protein powder
3 T. light honey
1/2 t. vanilla
1/4 t. artificial rum flavoring
dash salt
pinch nutmeg

1 1/2 frozen bananas

 Place water, barley milk and protein powder in blender and process until smooth. Add all remaining ingredients in order given.

 Add one or two of the following per serving (opt.):
1 1/2 t. flaxseed oil
1/4 t. acidophilus powder
1/8 t. vitamin C powder

 Blend until smooth and creamy. For thickest smoothies, keep blending time to a minimum.

Makes 3 cups. Serves 2. Serving Size 12 oz.

Calories	748
Fat	1g
Carbohydrate	123g
Protein	72.6g
Potassium	814mg
Vitamin C	15mg
Fiber	9.1g

MANDARIN TANGERINE FREEZE

1/2 c. Dole 100% Mandarin Tangerine juice concentrate
1/2 c. water
2/3 c. rice milk
2 T. Better Than Milk tofu powder
1/2 t. vanilla
1 large frozen banana
12 ice cubes

 Place rice milk (or your choice of any other milk or non-dairy substitute) and all remaining ingredients in blender in order given. **Note:** Dole Mandarin Tangerine juice concentrate is hard to find, but worth the effort. Regular orange juice concentrate can be substituted, if desired.

 Add one or two of the following per serving (opt.):
1 1/2 t. flaxseed oil
1/4 t. acidophilus powder
1/8 t. vitamin C powder

 Blend until smooth and creamy. For thickest smoothies, keep blending time to a minimum.

Makes 4 1/2 cups. Serves 3. Serving Size 12 oz.

Calories	151
Fat	.5g
Carbohydrate	35.1g
Protein	2.4g
Potassium	469mg
Vitamin C	25mg
Fiber	1.3g

DOUBLE TOFU BANANA

1/2 c. water
1/2 c. rice milk
1/2 c. Welch's 100% White Grape Peach concentrate
2 T. Better Than Milk tofu powder
1" slice lite tofu
1/2 t. vanilla
2 frozen bananas
10 ice cubes

Place rice milk (or your choice of any other milk or non-dairy substitute) and all remaining ingredients in blender in order given. (If adding protein powder, add first and blend with liquid.)

Add one or two of the following per serving (opt.):
1/2 T. rice protein powder
1 1/2 t. flaxseed oil
1/4 t. acidophilus powder
1/8 t. vitamin C powder

Blend until smooth and creamy. For thickest smoothies, keep blending time to a minimum.

Makes 4 1/2 cups. Serves 3. Serving Size 12 oz.

Calories	216
Fat	.9g
Carbohydrate	49.8g
Protein	3.3g
Potassium	301mg
Vitamin C	54mg
Fiber	1.8g

HAWAIIAN FRUIT DELIGHT

1/2 c. barley milk
1 1/3 c. pineapple juice
1/4 t. pineapple extract
1/2 t. coconut extract
1/8 t. orange extract
1/2 c. Dole Pineapple Orange concentrate
1/2 c. fresh or frozen pineapple chunks

1 t. vanilla
1 frozen banana
8 ice cubes

Place barley milk (or your choice of any other milk or non-dairy substitute) and all remaining ingredients in blender in order given. (If adding protein powder, add first and blend with liquid.)

Add one or two of the following per serving (opt.):
1/2 T. rice protein powder
1 1/2 t. flaxseed oil
1/4 t. acidophilus powder
1 t. sunflower seeds

Blend until smooth and creamy. For thickest smoothies, keep blending time to a minimum.

Makes 4 1/2 cups. Serves 3. Serving Size 12 oz.

Calories 198
Fat 2g
Carbohydrate .. 48.8g
Protein 2.3g
Potassium 555mg
Vitamin C 72mg
Fiber 2.9g

BANANA MILK

1 1/4 c. barley milk
2-4 T. apple juice concentrate, or to taste
1 t. vanilla
2 ripe bananas
1" slice lite tofu
few sprinkles nutmeg
8 ice cubes

Place barley milk (or your choice of any other milk or non-dairy substitute) and all remaining ingredients in blender in order given.

Add one or two of the following per serving (opt.):
1/4 t. acidophilus powder
1/8 t. vitamin C powder
1 T. chopped almonds

Blend until smooth and creamy. For thickest smoothies, keep blending time to a minimum.

Makes 4 1/2 cups. Serves 3. Serving Size 12 oz.

Calories 175
Fat 8g
Carbohydrate .. 39.5g
Protein 4.1g
Potassium 444mg
Vitamin C 31mg
Fiber 3.9g

TROPICAL SMOOTHIES

HI-PROTEIN SPICY BANANA

1/2 c. water
1/2 c. oat milk
1/2 t. vanilla
1 t. sesame seeds
1 T. raw sunflower seeds
2/3 c. frozen apple juice concentrate
2 T. Better Than Milk tofu powder
1/8 t. cinnamon

1/8 t. nutmeg
1 1/4" slice lite tofu
2 frozen bananas
12 ice cubes

 Place water and oat milk (or your choice of any other milk or non-dairy substitute) and all remaining ingredients in blender in order given. (If adding protein powder, add first and blend with liquid.)

 Add one or two of the following per serving (opt.):
1/2 T. rice protein powder
1 1/2 t. flaxseed oil
1/4 t. acidophilus powder

 Blend until smooth and creamy. For thickest smoothies, keep blending time to a minimum.

Makes 6 cups. Serves 4. Serving Size 12 oz.

Calories 200
Fat 1.9g
Carbohydrate .. 45.1g
Protein 2.1g
Potassium 564mg
Vitamin C 55mg
Fiber 2.4g

MANGO BERRY

1/2 c. barley milk
1/2 c. water
1 fresh banana
1 c. fresh mango chunks
1/4 c. fresh or frozen raspberries
4 ice cubes
1/2 c. Dole Pineapple Orange Strawberry concentrate

Place barley milk (or your choice of any other milk or non-dairy substitute), water and all remaining ingredients in blender in order given. (If adding protein powder, add first and blend with liquid.)

Add one or two of the following per serving (opt.):
1/2 T. rice protein powder
1 1/2 t. flaxseed oil
1/4 t. acidophilus powder
1 t. sunflower seeds

Blend until smooth and creamy. For thickest smoothies, keep blending time to a minimum.

Makes 3 cups. Serves 2. Serving Size 12 oz.

Calories	273
Fat	.6g
Carbohydrate	67.7g
Protein	3.1g
Potassium	798mg
Vitamin C	91mg
Fiber	5.1g

TROPICAL 🍍 SMOOTHIES

MANGO CREAM

1/4 c. water
1/4 c. oat milk
1 T. protein powder
1 1/2 c. fresh mango chunks
1 c. frozen peach chunks
1/2 c. lite tofu
6 ice cubes

 Place water and oat milk (or your choice of any other milk or non-dairy substitute) and protein powder in blender and process until powder is no longer grainy. Add all remaining ingredients in blender in order given.

 Add one or two of the following per serving (opt.):
1 1/2 t. flaxseed oil
1/4 t. acidophilus powder
1/8 t. vitamin C powder

 Blend until smooth and creamy. For thickest smoothies, keep blending time to a minimum.

Makes 4 1/2 cups. Serves 3. Serving Size 12 oz.

Calories	113
Fat	.8g
Carbohydrate	21.5g
Protein	7.3g
Potassium	241mg
Vitamin C	27mg
Fiber	2.7g

MANGO PUDDING

3/4 c. Welch's 100% White Grape Peach concentrate
1/4 c. oat milk
2 1/2 c. fresh mango chunks
1 c. firm lite tofu
12 large ice cubes

 Place oat milk (or your choice of any other milk or non-dairy substitute) and all remaining ingredients in blender in order given. (If adding protein powder, add first and blend with liquid.)

 Add one or two of the following per serving (opt.):
1/2 T. rice protein powder
1 1/2 t. flaxseed oil
1/4 t. acidophilus powder
1/8 t. vitamin C powder

 Blend until smooth and creamy. For thickest smoothies, keep blending time to a minimum.

Makes 4 1/2 cups. Serves 3. Serving Size 12 oz.

Calories 317
Fat 1.4g
Carbohydrate .. 73.1g
Protein 5.7g
Potassium 215mg
Vitamin C 133mg
Fiber 2.5g

TROPICAL 🍍 SMOOTHIES

MANGO TANGO

Bonus: phosphorus, potassium, vitamins A and C

1 c. barley milk
1 fresh mango, cubed
1/2 c. grated apple
8 fresh or frozen strawberries
1/4 c. avocado chunks
1 frozen banana
1/4 t. vitamin C powder

Place barley milk (or your choice of any other milk or non-dairy substitute) and all remaining ingredients in blender in order given. (If adding protein powder, add first and blend with liquid.)

Add one or two of the following per serving (opt.):
1/2 T. rice protein powder
1 1/2 t. flaxseed oil
1/4 t. acidophilus powder
1/8 t. vitamin C powder

Blend until smooth and creamy. For thickest smoothies, keep blending time to a minimum.

Makes 4 1/2 cups. Serves 3. Serving Size 12 oz.

Calories 283
Fat 4.9g
Carbohydrate .. 62g
Protein 4.9g
Potassium 1089mg
Vitamin C 639mg
Fiber 14.6g

TROPICAL 🍍 SMOOTHIES

PINE-ORANGE FREEZE

Bonus: phosphorus, potassium, protein

1/4 c. oat milk
1/2 c. frozen apple juice concentrate
3/4 c. frozen orange juice concentrate
1 can (15 1/4 oz.) crushed pineapple in its own juice
3 T. tofu powder
1/3 c. lite tofu
10 ice cubes

Place oat milk (or your choice of any other milk or non-dairy substitute) and all remaining ingredients in blender in order given.

Add one or two of the following per serving (opt.):
1 1/2 t. flaxseed oil
1/4 t. acidophilus powder
1/8 t. vitamin C powder

Blend until smooth and creamy. For thickest smoothies, keep blending time to a minimum.

Makes 4 1/2 cups. Serves 3. Serving Size 12 oz.

Calories	366
Fat	.9g
Carbohydrate	85.7g
Protein	5.5g
Potassium	1071mg
Vitamin C	104mg
Fiber	1.8g

TROPICAL SMOOTHIES

WHITE GRAPE PEACH FREEZE

Bonus: phosphorus

1/2 c. water   10 ice cubes
1/2 c. rice milk
1/2 c. Welch's 100% White Grape Peach concentrate
2 T. Better Than Milk tofu powder
1/2 t. vanilla
1/2 c. frozen peach chunks
1 frozen banana

 Place rice milk (or your choice of any other milk or non-dairy substitute) and all remaining ingredients in blender in order given. (If adding protein powder, add first and blend with liquid.)

 Add one or two of the following per serving (opt.):
1/2 T. rice protein powder
1 1/2 t. flaxseed oil
1/4 t. acidophilus powder
1/8 t. vitamin C powder

 Blend until smooth and creamy. For thickest smoothies, keep blending time to a minimum.

Makes 4 1/2 cups. Serves 3. Serving Size 12 oz.

Calories	183
Fat	.4g
Carbohydrate	43.8g
Protein	1.4g
Potassium	206mg
Vitamin C	53mg
Fiber	1.5g

PAPAYA CREME

Bonus: phosphorus, calcium, vitamin A

1 1/4 c. Knudsen's Papaya Nectar
1/4 c. oat milk
1/4" slice firm lite tofu
2 small frozen bananas

Place oat milk (or your choice of any other milk or non-dairy substitute) and all remaining ingredients in blender in order given. (If adding protein powder, add first and blend with liquid.)

Add one or two of the following per serving (opt.):
1/2 T. rice protein powder
1 1/2 t. flaxseed oil
1/4 t. acidophilus powder
1/8 t. vitamin C powder

Blend until smooth and creamy. For thickest smoothies, keep blending time to a minimum.

Makes 3 cups. Serves 2. Serving Size 12 oz.

Calories	216
Fat	1g
Carbohydrate	54g
Protein	2.1g
Potassium	509mg
Vitamin C	16mg
Fiber	3.8g

PINEAPPLE-COCONUT COOLER

1/2 c. barley milk
1/4 c. Welch's 100% White Grape juice concentrate
1/3 c. pineapple juice concentrate
1/4 t. coconut extract
2 ripe pears
1/4" slice firm tofu
8 ice cubes

Place barley milk (or your choice of any other milk or non-dairy substitute) and all remaining ingredients in blender in order given. (If adding protein powder, add first and blend with liquid.)

Add one or two of the following per serving (opt.):
1/2 T. rice protein powder
1 1/2 t. flaxseed oil
1/4 t. acidophilus powder
1/8 t. vitamin C powder

Blend until smooth and creamy. For thickest smoothies, keep blending time to a minimum.

Makes 4 1/2 cups. Serves 3. Serving Size 12 oz.

Calories	200
Fat	.5g
Carbohydrate	49.1g
Protein	2g
Potassium	276mg
Vitamin C	74mg
Fiber	3.5g

PAPAYA-PINEAPPLE COOLER

Bonus: vitamin A

1/2 c. rice milk
1/4 c. Welch's 100% White Grape juice concentrate
1/3 c. pineapple juice concentrate
1 1/2 c. papaya chunks (or 3/4 c. papaya juice)
1 ripe pear
1/4" slice firm tofu
8 ice cubes

Place rice milk (or your choice of any other milk or non-dairy substitute) and all remaining ingredients in blender in order given. (If adding protein powder, add first and blend with liquid.)

Add one or two of the following per serving (opt.):
1/2 T. rice protein powder
1 1/2 t. flaxseed oil
1/4 t. acidophilus powder
1/8 t. vitamin C powder

Blend until smooth and creamy. For thickest smoothies, keep blending time to a minimum.

Makes 4 1/2 cups. Serves 3. Serving Size 12 oz.

Calories	195
Fat	.4g
Carbohydrate	47.6g
Protein	2.2g
Potassium	387mg
Vitamin C	116mg
Fiber	3.4g

TROPICANANNA

1 c. barley milk
2 T. Knudsen's Papaya Juice Concentrate
1/4 c. Welch's 100% White Grape juice concentrate
1/3 c. pineapple juice concentrate
1 ripe pear
1 frozen banana
1/4" slice firm tofu
8 ice cubes

 Place barley milk (or your choice of any other milk or non-dairy substitute) and all remaining ingredients in blender in order given. (If adding protein powder, add first and blend with liquid.)

 Add one or two of the following per serving (opt.):
1/2 T. rice protein powder
1 1/2 t. flaxseed oil
1/4 t. acidophilus powder
1/8 t. vitamin C powder

 Blend until smooth and creamy. For thickest smoothies, keep blending time to a minimum.

Makes 4 1/2 cups. Serves 3. Serving Size 12 oz.

Calories 227
Fat 5g
Carbohydrate . . 55.1g
Protein 2.8g
Potassium 375mg
Vitamin C 105mg
Fiber 3.9g

VEGGIE SMOOTHIES

Packed with nutrients for a filling snack!

How many times have you heard "eat your veggies!"? Well, now you have another option — you can DRINK your veggies!

Fruit and vegetable juices most often have the fiber removed, and fiber is absolutely essential to good health, but if you're eating whole grains and other unrefined foods, you will still get a good supply of fiber. The nutrients in these drinks more than make up for the lack of fiber. Besides, they're TONS better for you than a soda pop!

VERY VEGGIE

3 c. V8 juice
2 t. Worcestershire sauce
1/4 t. Tabasco sauce (opt)
1/2 c. ripe avocado
2 T. chopped red bell pepper
1 vegetable bouillon cube
1/8 t. pepper

1 T. lemon juice
3 ice cubes

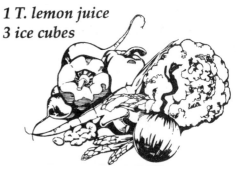

 Place all ingredients in blender in order given. (If adding protein powder, add first and blend with liquid.) Garnish with fresh parsley. If desired, serve over crushed ice.

 Add one or two of the following per serving (opt.):
1/2 T. rice protein powder
1 1/2 t. flaxseed oil
1/4 t. acidophilus powder
1/8 t. vitamin C powder

 Blend until smooth and creamy. For thickest smoothies, keep blending time to a minimum.

Makes 6 cups. Serves 4. Serving Size 12 oz.

Calories	86
Fat	4.6g
Carbohydrate	11.7g
Protein	1.8g
Potassium	558mg
Vitamin C	61mg
Fiber	3.3g

VITAVEGGIE
(Carotene Special)

1/4 c. Westsoy low fat soy milk
2/3 c. Knudsen Vita Juice
1/3 c. apple juice concentrate
1/4 c. canned pumpkin, unsweetened
6 ice cubes

Place soy milk (or your choice of any other milk or non-dairy substitute) and all remaining ingredients in blender in order given. (If adding protein powder, add first and blend with liquid.)

Add one or two of the following per serving (opt.):
1/2 T. rice protein powder
1 1/2 t. flaxseed oil
1/4 t. acidophilus powder
1/8 t. vitamin C powder

Blend until smooth and creamy. For thickest smoothies, keep blending time to a minimum.

Makes 3 cups. Serves 2. Serving Size 12 oz.

Calories	139
Fat	.1g
Carbohydrate	33g
Protein	1.4g
Potassium	333mg
Vitamin C	68mg
Fiber	1g

VEGGIE SMOOTHIES

RED RED VEGGIE

3/4 c. V8 juice
3/4 c. fresh carrot juice
1/4 c. celery juice
4 T. beet juice
1/2 t. vitamin C powder
14 ice cubes

Place all ingredients in blender in order given.

Add one or two of the following per serving (opt.):
1 1/2 t. flaxseed oil
1/4 t. acidophilus powder

Blend until smooth and creamy. For thickest smoothies, keep blending time to a minimum.

Makes 3 cups. Serves 2. Serving Size 12 oz.

Calories 52
Fat 3g
Carbohydrate .. 11.5g
Protein 1.4g
Potassium 471mg
Vitamin C 1195mg
Fiber 2.1g

PEAR OF CARROTS

1/3 c. soy milk
2 T. apple juice concentrate
1 3/4 c. fresh carrot juice
1 large pear, cored
1 sprig parsley
6 ice cubes

 Place soy milk (or your choice of any other milk or non-dairy substitute) and all remaining ingredients in blender in order given.

 Add one or two of the following per serving (opt.):
1 1/2 t. flaxseed oil
1/4 t. acidophilus powder
1/8 t. vitamin C powder

 Blend until smooth and creamy. For thickest smoothies, keep blending time to a minimum.

Makes 3 cups. Serves 2. Serving Size 12 oz.

Calories	237
Fat	2g
Carbohydrate	51.1g
Protein	8.9g
Potassium	1879mg
Vitamin C	61mg
Fiber	7.3g

GREEN GIANT

1/2 c. rice milk
1 c. fresh carrot juice
1 1/2 c. V8 juice
1 sprig parsley
6 large spinach leaves
1/4 t. tabasco
1/2" slice firm lite tofu (opt.)
6 ice cubes

 Place rice milk (or your choice of any other milk or non-dairy substitute) and all remaining ingredients in blender in order given.

 Add one or two of the following per serving (opt.):
1 1/2 t. flaxseed oil
1/4 t. acidophilus powder
1/8 t. vitamin C powder

 Blend until smooth and creamy. For thickest smoothies, keep blending time to a minimum.

Makes 3 cups. Serves 2. Serving Size 12 oz.

Calories	213
Fat	2.5g
Carbohydrate	41g
Protein	15g
Potassium	2751mg
Vitamin C	136mg
Fiber	10.3g

CREOLE VEGGIE

2 c. V8 juice
1/2 c. fresh carrot juice
1 t. tabasco
1 t. lemon juice
4 spinach leaves
1 medium sprig parsley
12 ice cubes

 Place all ingredients in blender in order given. (If adding protein powder, add first and blend with liquid.)

 Add one or two of the following per serving (opt.):
1/2 T. rice protein powder
1 t. sunflower seeds
1/4 t. acidophilus powder
1/8 t. vitamin C powder

 Blend until smooth and creamy. For thickest smoothies, keep blending time to a minimum.

Makes 3 cups. Serves 2. Serving Size 12 oz.

Calories 167
Fat 2.1g
Carbohydrate .. 32.7g
Protein 13.1g
Potassium 2555mg
Vitamin C 153mg
Fiber 9.6g

VEGGIE SMOOTHIES

ALOHA CARROT

1/4 c. rice milk
1 1/2 c. fresh carrot juice
2 T. pineapple juice concentrate
1/2" slice firm lite tofu
1 frozen banana
6 ice cubes

Place rice milk (or your choice of any other milk or non-dairy substitute) and all remaining ingredients in blender in order given. (If adding protein powder, add first and blend with liquid.)

Add one or two of the following per serving (opt.):
1/2 T. rice protein powder
1 1/2 t. flaxseed oil
1/4 t. acidophilus powder
1/8 t. vitamin C powder

Blend until smooth and creamy. For thickest smoothies, keep blending time to a minimum.

Makes 3 cups. Serves 2. Serving Size 12 oz.

Calories	153
Fat	.8g
Carbohydrate	34.5g
Protein	3.4g
Potassium	773mg
Vitamin C	34mg
Fiber	3.1g

VEGGIE SMOOTHIES

CAROTENE SURPRISE

1/2 c. rice milk
1 c. carrot juice
2 T. pineapple juice concentrate
2 frozen bananas

 Place rice milk (or your choice of any other milk or non-dairy substitute) and all remaining ingredients in blender in order given.

 Add one or two of the following per serving (opt.):
1 1/2 t. flaxseed oil
1/4 t. acidophilus powder
1/8 t. vitamin C powder

 Blend until smooth and creamy. For thickest smoothies, keep blending time to a minimum.

Makes 3 cups. Serves 2. Serving Size 12 oz.

Calories	125
Fat	.5g
Carbohydrate	30.4g
Protein	1.7g
Potassium	559mg
Vitamin C	25mg
Fiber	2.6g

VEGGIE SMOOTHIES

RED SUNSET

Juicer Recipe

These raw ingredients combine to form a zesty energy booster.

8 large carrots
3 red apples
1/2" slice raw beet
1 sprig parsley
1/2" slice ginger root

Scrub chilled carrots and beets and cut off tops.
Juice all ingredients together in a Champion juicer.

Stir in one or two of the following per serving (opt.):
1/4 t. acidophilus powder
1/8 t. vitamin C powder

If desired, serve over crushed ice.

Makes 3 cups. Serves 2. Serving Size 12 oz.

Calories	213
Fat	1.9g
Carbohydrate	45.2g
Protein	8.5g
Potassium	1912mg
Vitamin C	42mg
Fiber	5.8g

VEGGIE  SMOOTHIES

RASPBERRY GINGERSNAP

Juicer Recipe

1/3 c. Welch's 100% White Grape Raspberry concentrate
10 carrots
3 red apples
1/2" slice raw beet
1/4" slice raw ginger root
16 ice cubes

 Juice all fruits and veggies in a Champion juicer. Place juice in blender and add raspberry concentrate and ice cubes.

 Add one or two of the following per serving (opt.):
1 1/2 t. flaxseed oil
1/4 t. acidophilus powder
1/8 t. vitamin C powder

 Blend until smooth.

Makes 4 1/2 cups. Serves 3. Serving Size 12 oz.

Calories	158
Fat	.4g
Carbohydrate	36.7g
Protein	1.3g
Potassium	564mg
Vitamin C	36mg
Fiber	2g

CARROT APPLE SPECIAL
Juicer Recipe

12 carrots
3 red apples
1/2 c. apple juice concentrate
20 ice cubes

 After juicing carrots and apples, place juice in blender and add apple juice concentrate and ice.

Add one or two of the following per serving (opt.):
1 1/2 t. flaxseed oil
1/4 t. acidophilus powder
1/8 t. vitamin C powder

Blend until smooth.

Makes 4 1/2 cups. Serves 3 Serving Size 12 oz.

Calories	284
Fat	1.1g
Carbohydrate	69.3g
Protein	3.2g
Potassium	1286mg
Vitamin C	82mg
Fiber	12.4g

MILKS FOR SMOOTHIES

from Grains, Nuts and Seeds

You can purchase non-dairy "milks" from the health food store, or make your own using these recipes. If you use dairy products, you can use regular milk in any of the recipes in this book.

Many people have allergies or sensitivities to cow's milk and all products made from milk. Most childhood ear infections can be eliminated if dairy products are avoided. In 30 years of raising 5 children, we only had 3 ear infections, and that was at a time when we used dairy products on a regular basis! Most snorers are able to sleep soundly (and quietly!) when dairy products are avoided.

I grind my own grains, seeds and nuts in my electric grain mill, blender, or seed mill. I usually grind a quart at a time and refrigerate.

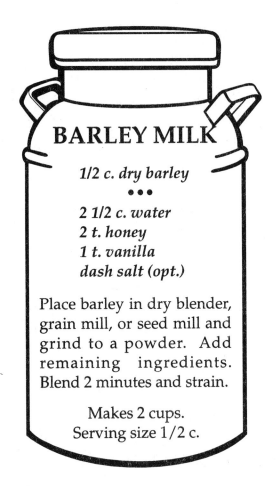

BARLEY MILK

1/2 c. dry barley

• • •

2 1/2 c. water
2 t. honey
1 t. vanilla
dash salt (opt.)

Place barley in dry blender, grain mill, or seed mill and grind to a powder. Add remaining ingredients. Blend 2 minutes and strain.

Makes 2 cups.
Serving size 1/2 c.

Cal. 100, Fat 0g, Carb. 22.5g, Pro. 3g, Pot. 72mg, Vit. C 0mg, Fib. 3g

Barley milk is our favorite because of its creamy texture. Barley flour can be purchased or ordered in health stores. Barley milk is not yet available. Milk lasts 2-3 days in refrigerator.

Sprouted Barley Milk: Use 1 c. 3-day sprouted barley and process as above, omitting honey.

Excellent in smoothies, cooking and baking, on cereal, or for drinking.

OAT MILK

1/2 c. oat flour
2 c. water
2 t. honey
1 t. vanilla
1 1/2 T. apple juice
    concentrate
dash salt (opt.)

Place all ingredients in blender jar. Blend 1 minute and strain.

Makes 2 cups.
Serving size 1/2 c.

Cal. 67, Fat 1g, Carb. 13g, Pro. 2g, Pot. 67mg, Vit. C 7mg, Fib. 2g

Oat milk is easy to find in health stores, but a lot cheaper to make at home from whole oats (called oat "groats") or oat flour. Milk lasts 2-3 days in refrigerator.

Excellent in smoothies, cooking and baking, on cereal, or for drinking.

RICE MILK

1/2 c. brown rice
2 c. water
2 t. honey
1 t. vanilla
dash salt (opt.)

Place rice in dry blender, grain mill or seed mill and grind to a powder. Combine with remaining ingredients. Blend 2 minutes and strain.

Makes 2 cups.
Serving size 1/2 c.

Cal. 84, Fat 1g, Carb. 18g, Pro. 2g, Pot. 59mg, Vit. C 0mg, Fib. 1g

Milk lasts 2-3 days in refrigerator.

Brown rice is higher in fiber, B vitamins and trace minerals than white rice. Rice flour and rice milk are available in health food stores.

Excellent in smoothies, cooking and baking, on cereal, or for drinking.

NUT MILK

1/2 c. whole almonds
2 1/2 c. water
2 t. honey
1 t. vanilla
dash salt (opt.)

Place nuts in dry blender or seed mill and grind to a powder. Combine with remaining ingredients. Blend 1 minute.

Makes 2 cups.
Serving size 1/2 c.

Cal. 115, Fat 9.3g, Carb. 6.5g, Pro. 3.6g, Pot. 132mg, Vit. C 0mg, Fib. 1.9g

This milk can be used in smoothies, or strained for drinking. Milk lasts 2-3 days in refrigerator.

Almond Milk is available in health food stores. Other nuts, such as cashews or hazelnuts also make excellent milks. Nut milks are higher in fat than grain milks, but not too much if you're not using oil in cooking.

Excellent in smoothies, cooking and baking, on cereal, or for drinking.

SMOOTHIE "MILKS"

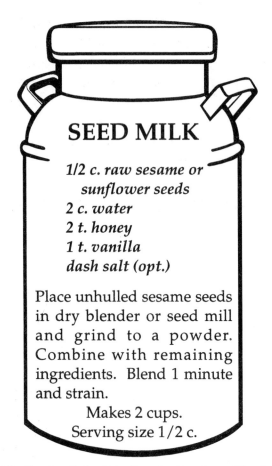

SEED MILK

1/2 c. raw sesame or
*   sunflower seeds*
2 c. water
2 t. honey
1 t. vanilla
dash salt (opt.)

Place unhulled sesame seeds in dry blender or seed mill and grind to a powder. Combine with remaining ingredients. Blend 1 minute and strain.

Makes 2 cups.
Serving size 1/2 c.

Sesame: Cal. 102, Fat 8g, Carb. 4.5g, Pro. 4g, Pot. 2mg, Vit. C 0mg, Fib. 2g
Sunflower: Cal. 116, Fat 9.5g, Carb. 6.5g, Pro. 2.9g, Pot. 84mg, Vit. C 0mg, Fib. 1g

Milk lasts 2-3 days in refrigerator.

Unhulled sesame seeds (the brown ones) are higher in fiber, calcium, iron and trace minerals than processed white seeds.

Excellent in smoothies, cooking and baking. This milk's stronger flavor makes it a little **too** strong for drinking.

INFORMATION

*In this section, you'll find valuable information about foods and their con-
nection to wellness. Health can be improved by eating "whole"some
foods, drinking lots of pure water, getting adequate exercise (preferably in
clean, fresh air), developing a good positive attitude, and learning to be
less stressed.*

*Good health is your most valuable resource, and it IS within your power
to feel better than you do right now.*

QUESTIONS AND ANSWERS

DO SMOOTHIES ADD TOO MANY EXTRA CALORIES?

1-2-3 Smoothies contain only essential calories from whole fruits and juices... the ones we're supposed to be consuming on a daily basis. Remember the "five servings a day" USRDA recommendation for fruits and veggies? Are you the one in three who actually follows this advice?

Be honest now...how many days a week do you ACTUALLY eat the minimum requirement of two fruits and three veggies? Smoothies to the rescue! With approximately 2 fruits (or vegetables) and one 8 oz. serving of juice in each frosty beverage, it's easy to get a full

> How many days a week do you ACTUALLY eat the *minimum* requirement of two fruits and three veggies?

day's supply of many nutrients, including the important antioxidant, vitamin C.

In an average serving, if you add flavored yogurt, the calories in your smoothie increase from 220 to 350, and fat increases from less than 1 gram to 8.3 grams. If you add ice cream, the calories skyrocket from approximately 220 to 490!!, and fat jumps to a whopping 15 grams.

HOW MANY SMOOTHIES A DAY?

One fruit smoothie per day is ideal for a growing body, or for a power-packed meal replacement. For weight *loss*, use 1-2 vegetable smoothies (fortified with protein, food enzyme supplements in the form of pow-

 dered juice (available in capsules), vitamin C and essential fatty acids) per day in place of meals, then have a low-fat meal packed with high-fiber grains, beans, raw vegetables and fruit.

For weight *gain*, add extra vegetable-based protein powder and drink up to 2 smoothies per day as a snack. It is not necessary or advisable to add animal fat or protein to promote weight gain. Research has shown that body weight normalizes when fed a wide variety of nourishing high-fiber foods (animal products have NO fiber!). For extra calories, add raisins, dates, nuts and seeds.

CAN THOSE WITH HYPOGLYCEMIA, DIABETES, OR CHRONIC FATIGUE SYNDROME DRINK SMOOTHIES?

Any person with a tendency toward low blood sugar should limit fruit juices to no more than three servings per week, and those should be diluted with part water. An excess of fruit juices can be harmful because it causes a rapid rise in blood sugar, which will then plummet as insulin is over secreted in the body's effort to deal with the sweets. **SOLUTION:** Use a powdered juice product with the sugar removed. The one I use contains fiber and powdered enzymes...an excellent alternative when I'm too busy to do my own juicing!

IS INDIGESTION A PROBLEM?

Rather than taking over-the-counter medications, try eating more raw foods and foods lower in fat. Usually, it's the burgers and pizzas you eat "on the run" that cause the gas, abdominal pain, heartburn, bloating and nausea. If you're in that big of a hurry, grab a smoothie instead! You'll LOVE the results.

BABY SMOOTHIES??

During baby's first six months, breast milk, the only source of essential nutrients and protective elements, is best. At around six to nine months, fresh fruit or vegetable smoothies can be given to a baby who shows interest in other foods. Start with one fruit or vegetable at a time to test baby's tolerance. Smoothies should be made with only whole blended fruit or juiced vegetables. They can be placed in a cup or in a baby's bottle with a cross-cut nipple. Serve at room temperature. Fruit juice concentrates should be limited or avoided, as they would taste too sweet to a baby or a young child (unless mixed with an equal amount of purified water).

Add-ins, like adult-sized portions of protein powder and additional vitamins, minerals, and supplements should not be used, except in "failure to thrive" cases where this might be the only way to supply essential nutrients. Be sure to consult with your pediatrician.

I'M ALLERGIC TO DAIRY PRODUCTS. HOW CAN I BE SURE TO GET ENOUGH CALCIUM?

Calcium is a mineral which occurs naturally in the earth. It is a macromineral, meaning we need larger amounts of it than microminerals, trace minerals, meaning we need just a tiny *trace* of each one. Studies have shown that a deficiency of trace minerals is often responsible for the lack of calcium in the body. It's not that we're not getting **enough** calcium—we're just not getting enough trace minerals for calcium to be absorbed and utilized. Trace minerals and calcium are present in proper quantities in whole foods, especially in herbs, like Dr. Christopher's "CalcTea". Refined foods are stripped of trace minerals.

Is it possible to get the recommended 1000 mg. of calcium if you're not eating dairy products? Let's see.... You could eat 28 oranges, 150 apples, 26 cantaloupes! There's something wrong with this picture! If the "recommended" amount is greater than we can obtain from foods we eat, even without dairy products, there's something wrong with the recommended amount!!!

People living in countries where very few, if any, animal products, including dairy, are consumed have good strong bones...without calcium supplementation. Recent studies show excess protein causes the calcium to be forced from the bones and out of the body. To me, that explains why Americans, as a milk-drinking, meat-eating people have so much osteoporosis. Calcium also helps keep us **calm.** **Anyone** stressed out???

I'VE HEARD THAT VITAMIN C IS A GOOD ANTIOXIDANT. HOW MUCH CAN I ADD TO A SMOOTHIE?

You can get a full day's supply (60 mg RDA) of vitamin C (ascorbic acid) from just 3/4 c. strawberries, 1 orange, 1/2 of a papaya, or 1 kiwi. With recent research showing how powerful vitamin C is at scavenging for free radicals, helping with any healing, relieving pain, etc., Dr. Balch recommends 3,000 mg. That would be 36 cups of strawberries, 43 oranges, 16 papayas, or 41 kiwis. OR, you could add several capsules of a powdered juice product (with fiber and powdered enzymes added to it) to any smoothie—

> Vitamin C is an powerful antioxidant for scavenging cancer-causing free radicals.

with no change in flavor. It is ALWAYS best to get nutrients from WHOLE foods, not from isolated vitamins and minerals.

IF FIBER IS SO IMPORTANT, WHY IS THERE SO LITTLE FIBER IN THESE RECIPES?

Fiber is a form of carbohydrate and is absolutely essential for good health. Only PLANTS contain fiber, and fruits have the least of all. Fiber, often referred to as "roughage," because very little of it is digested or metabolized by the body, is essential in moving foods along in the digestive and elimination processes. Fiber acts like a sponge to retain water, resulting in softer, bulkier stools that prevent constipation and help keep the colon clean. This reduces the risk of colon cancer and other serious diseases. In addition, a high-fiber diet (at least 25-35 grams of fiber per day) interferes with the production of cholesterol, reducing the risk of heart disease. SO, be sure and get your daily dose of fiber from whole grains and vegetables.

DO CARBOHYDRATES CAUSE WEIGHT GAIN?

Refined carbohydrates are responsible for most weight gain. However, massive amounts of **complex** carbohydrates from grains and/or starchy vegetables can also cause weight gain. A balance of fresh vegetables, particularly the dark orange, red, and green leafy ones, is essential because these are processed most efficiently by the body.

Processed or refined carbohydrates (white flour, white bread, white sugar, and most commercial baked goods) are called (harmful) simple carbohydrates and are processed very quickly through the body. This results in roller coaster glucose levels, and can lead to and irritate such disorders as diabetes and hypoglycemia. The body stores most of the energy gained from these processed foods foods as FAT. **Whole** grains, fruits and vegetables are processed more slowly, resulting in even glucose levels and a constant energy supply that can be *used* by the body, rather than stored.

> Simple carbohydrates are found in fruits. Complex carbohydrates are found in vegetables, whole grains and legumes.

Helpful *simple carbohydrates* are found in fruits. (Eating too much fruit **can** cause weight gain, even if it is whole, raw fruit. Again, a good balance is essential.) *Complex carbohydrates* are found in vegetables, whole grains and legumes and have more complex chains of molecules - like a single strand of sewing thread as compared to a heavy braided rope. This more complex chain is made up of fiber and starches. It takes the body a while to convert **complex** carbohydrates into glucose to use for energy or store for the future. This delay in processing allows the body to slowly, calmly go about its business of utilizing valuable nutrients, without having to deal with any highs or lows in blood sugar like those created when refined simple carbohydrates are consumed.

For most people, it is recommended that at least half of the daily calorie intake be in the form of carbohydrates, most of them complex. Whole fruits and juices are usually higher in calories than vegetables, so they are an important source of carbohydrates.

ARE THIN PEOPLE HEALTHY?

Most people think wellness has *everything* to do with being thin. Why is it then that some people can carry extra pounds and feel "well" their whole lives while many thin people suffer from an endless string of health problems?

While excess weight is definitely hard on the body, some bodies are able to handle the extra pounds better than others. Why? It is because some are blessed with stronger bodies than others; some have inherently strong immune systems; some have both, but most of us have an average amount of both.

It takes a lot of effort to maintain the level of wellness we're born with and even more to improve on it. With today's busy lifestyle, who has time? We all have the *same* amount of time. It is up to each one of us to decide how well we will care for the bodies we've been given. We have an obligation to feel our best so we can live up to our potential, each doing our part to make this world a better place in which to live.

Much is written about each of the areas that make up wellness and each is equally important. Without paying attention to the total health picture, you will find yourself out of balance and feeling less than your best, because wellness is balance. Wellness is about finding out how to choose wisely the things we become involved in and putting the rest on the back burner and eliminating excess "should do's" all together. (Most of my life, I didn't know it was alright to HAVE back burners, and now I keep losing them!)

> Take time to take care of yourself. No one else is going to do it for you!

Take the time to take care of yourself. No one else is going to do it for you! It's taken me nearly half a century to learn that I am worth the effort it takes to take care of my body. I hope this knowledge comes easier to you. If not, start now and learn to evaluate what your body needs to feel "WELL." ♥

ANTIOXIDANTS AND FREE RADICALS

We hear a lot about antioxidants these days, mostly in advertisements for CoQ_{10}, Ginkgo Biloba, Grape Seed Extract, Green Tea, Melatonin and Pycnogenol, enticing us to take this pill or that capsule to help protect the body from the formation of free radicals— atoms (alone or in groups) that can cause cell damage and lead to degenerative diseases such as cancer.

> The more refined, processed, fried foods, and especially fats you eat, the more free radicals your body produces.

Free radicals keep the immune system from functioning properly. What you may not realize is that the more refined, processed, fried foods, and especially fats you eat, the more free radicals your body produces and the more antioxidants you need to destroy those free radicals.

Antioxidants are made up of vitamins, minerals and enzymes. They occur naturally in whole foods. When we strip our foods of their nutrients, leaving them in an "unwhole" state, and damage the natural fats in foods by excess heat and processing (hydrogenating) them, we create free radicals. Radiation, pollution from any source (including cigarette smoke), chemicals in and on our foods, in our soils and in meats and nearly all processed foods are all responsible for creating free radicals.

Basically, the more we DO to our food, the more free radicals we allow to be created in our bodies. When we eat raw, whole foods and their juices, we supply antioxidant scavengers to destroy the free radicals. Free radicals are the **BAD GUYS** ! Antioxidants are the GOOD GUYS!!

In addition, stress (both good AND bad stress!!) **causes** the formation of free radicals. Stress **definitely** suppresses the immune system, further limiting the body's ability to use its naturally occurring free radical scavengers. It's a vicious cycle!

Free radical are also produced during exercise! and in the digestion of food. Overexercising is harmful. Overeating is harmful (in more ways than one!). No, the solution is NOT to stop both, but to do both in moderation.

What's the best solution? **Back to Basics!** Change to a high-fiber diet of whole grains, raw fruits, sprouts and green leafy vegetables. If you need to add additional antioxidants (and almost everyone does, especially when processed foods are consumed), smoothies are the perfect solution. When you use fresh, raw, whole foods, and fortify them with Juice Plus+, a powdered juice product (with the fiber and powdered enzymes added to it), you have a complete meal, or a power-packed snack.❤

> What's the best solution? Back to the BASICS—a high-fiber diet of whole foods and Juice Plus+ with active enzymes!

HOW TO SWITCH
TO A MORE "NATURAL" DIET

Most of us recognize the need to get "back to basics" with more unprocessed whole grains, legumes, fresh fruits and vegetables, but if you're like me, you want to know WHY?! When my children were growing up, "because I said so" didn't carry much weight at my house, but they (almost) always ate whatever I prepared when I told them what nutrients it supplied and what those nutrients' jobs were in their bodies. This turns the sometimes boring science of nutrition into an interesting science project!

> What child wouldn't love a whole grain cookie and a smoothie for breakfast?

What child wouldn't love a whole-grain cookie (filled with nuts, seeds and raisins or dates, of course) and a smoothie (filled with fruit, protein powder, and a full day's supply of vitamin C and other add-in nutrients) for breakfast? How about pita pockets (filled with cracked wheat or brown rice salad) for lunch? Veggieburgers with white sauce (non-dairy, made with white beans) for dinner? "Natural" foods don't need to be boring. Yes, it takes more time and effort, but not more time and effort than keeping up with illnesses and diseases.

Cooking with the basics is a whole new adventure. Prevention is a LOT more fun than dealing with sickness and searching for cures. My cookbooks, *Natural* **Meals In Minutes** and **Country Beans** and my video "Quick, Wholesome Foods," are filled with hundreds of quick low-fat recipes using the basics—unprocessed grains, legumes, seeds, nuts, fruits and veggies.

The chart on the next page will help you learn to combine the basics to meet your protein needs.

PROTEIN COMBINING CHART

Take a look at the two types of protein available in foods:

(1) Proteins from Animal Sources, and (2) Proteins from Plant Sources.

Proteins from Animal Sources are complete proteins by themselves; however, economical Plant Sources can be combined to make a complete, better quality protein that is rich in fiber, vitamins and minerals... with NO cholesterol. It's easy to eat little or no meat and still achieve your daily protein requirement by combining foods from plant sources found in the chart below, which lists the most common varieties.

Using the circular chart, combine one food from *any* two groups.

Whole Grains

Amaranth
Barley*
Buckwheat*
Corn
Millet
Oats*
Quinoa*
Brown Rice
Rye*
Spelt*
Triticale*
Wheat*

Nuts, Seeds

Alfalfa Seeds*
Almonds*
Broccoli Seeds*
Cabbage Seeds
Cashews
Clover Seeds*
Filberts*
Flax Seeds
Pecans
Pine Nuts
Poppy Seeds
Pumpkin Seeds
Radish Seeds*
Brown Sesame Seeds
Sunflower Seeds*
Walnuts

Legumes

Anasazi Beans
Appaloosa Beans
Adzuki Beans*
Black Beans
Black Lentils*
Blackeyed Peas*
Calypso Beans
Cannelini Beans
Fava Beans
Garbanzo Beans*
Great Northern
Green Lentils*
Green Peas*
Kidney Beans
Lima Beans
Mung Beans*
Navy Beans
Pea Beans
Peanuts
Pink Beans
Pinto Beans
Red Beans
Red Lentils*
Rice Beans
Scarlet Runner Beans
Small White Beans
Soy Beans
Tofu & Soy Products
Yellow Peas*

Note: Vegetables (especially green, leafy ones) combine well with ANY of these groups. Be sure to eat **at least** 4 servings *(1/2 c. cooked or 1 c. raw leafy)* each day.

*These are my favorites to sprout and eat raw.

Here are a few examples of some simple meatless dishes that contain amino acids which the body will combine into a complete protein:

GRAINS + LEGUMES
Grain and
Garden Burger

GRAINS + SEEDS
Whole Wheat
Sunflower Seed Bread

GRAINS + NUTS
Fried Rice with Veggies
and Slivered Almonds

NUTS + GRAINS
Almond Milk on Cereal

NUTS + LEGUMES
Almond Tofu Stir Fry

SEEDS + GRAINS
Popped Seed Trail Mix

SEEDS + LEGUMES
Sunflower Seed Sprouts
and Red Lentil Sprouts
on Lettuce Leaves

LEGUMES + GRAINS
Crispy Wheat Crackers 5-Minute Bean Dip

LEGUMES + NUTS
Mung Bean Pasta Salad with Pine Nuts

LEGUMES + SEEDS
Creamy Bean Soup with
Flax Seed Bread

Now doesn't that seem uncomplicated and downright do-able? All it takes is a little planning to make sure you have lots of nutritious ingredients on hand. Give it a try! ❤

MOST COMMON SMOOTHIE FRUITS AND WHAT THEY'RE GOOD FOR

Apples (Juice)

calcium
phosphorus
potassium
vitamin A

Apricots

calcium
phosphorus
high in potassium
very high in vitamin A

Avocados

high in fatty acids
calcium
phosphorus
very high in potassium
very high in vitamin A
thiamine
riboflavin
niacin

Bananas

calcium
phosphorus *(bananas are touted for potassium, but are the same as an orange or grapefruit, less than blackberries)*
potassium
vitamin A

Blackberries

calcium
phosphorus
vitamin A
potassium
ascorbic Acid

Blueberries

phosphorus
potassium
vitamin A

Cantaloupe

phosphorus
calcium
very high in potassium
very high in vitamin A
high in vitamin C

Dates

high in potassium

Grape Juice

potassium
calcium
phosphorus
vitamin A
vitamin C

Honeydew

good source of potassium

Kiwi

high in vitamin A
calcium
phosphorus
good source of potassium
vitamin C *higher than either
lemons or oranges!*

Lemon

potassium
vitamin A
vitamin C

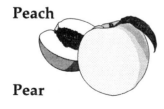

Mango

calcium
phosphorus
high in potassium
8000 IU vitamin A!
vitamin C

Nectarine

good source of potassium
good source of vitamin A

Orange

good source of calcium
phosphorus
potassium
vitamin A
vitamin C

Papaya

calcium
phosphorus
potassium
good source of vitamin A
vitamin C

Peach

phosphorus
potassium
vitamin A

Pear

calcium
phosphorus
potassium

Pineapple

potassium
vitamin A
vitamin C

Raisins
super high in potassium
high in phosphorus
calcium

Raspberries
calcium
phosphorus
potassium
vitamin A
vitamin C

Strawberries
calcium
phosphorus
potassium
vitamin A
vitamin C

Tangerines
calcium
potassium
good source of vitamin A
vitamin C

Watermelon
calcium
phosphorus
good potassium
high in vitamin A
vitamin C ❤

Nutritive Value of Foods, U.S. Dept. of Agriculture, 1981.

U.S.RDA

These are the Recommended Daily Dietary Allowances (RDA) for a HEALTHY person in the US consuming 2000 calories per day.

NUTRIENT	Amount Needed: 23-50 yr old woman or child 1-8 yrs
Protein	44 grams
Calcium	1000 milligrams
Phosphorus	800 mg
Iron	18 mg
Vitamin A	4000 IU
Vitamin C (ascorbic acid)	60 mg
Thiamin	1 mg
Riboflavin	1.2 mg
Niacin	13 mg

> The U.S. RDA is for "healthy" people, but most people are far from healthy.

I have talked with *thousands* of people in the last 30 years, and I haven't ever found one who thought he or she was really "healthy." Everyone was looking for something better, especially as they got busier and/or older. No one seemed to have enough energy, even with a diet high in calories. Very few thought they could manage without illnesses requiring several doctor's visits each year.

According to Dr. James Balch, author of **Prescription for Nutritional Healing,** the nutrient chart below, with much larger dosages and many more nutrients than the one above, gives a more realistic picture of what's actually needed by the body. Because we eat so many refined foods and so few fresh, whole grains, legumes, fruits and vegetables, Dr. Balch is probably right. BUT, each nutrient has a specific role in overall health, so who has **enough** knowledge to choose which ones our bodies do or don't need and formulate a pill that will provide the proper amounts for anyone taking it?

VITAMINS	DAILY DOSAGES
Vitamin A	10,000 IU
Beta-carotene	15,000 IU
Vitamin B1 (thiamine)	50 mg
Vitamin B2 (riboflavin)	50 mg
Vitamin B3 (niacinamide)	100 mg
Pantothenic acid (B5)	100 mg
Vitamin B6 (pyridoxine)	50 mg
Vitamin B12	300 mcg
Biotin	300 mcg
Choline	100 mg
Folic acid	800 mcg
Inositol	100 mg
Para-aminobenzoic acid (PABA)	50 mg
Vitamin C with mineral ascorbates	3,000 mg
Bioflavinoids (mixed)	500 mg
Hesperidin	100 mg
Rutin	25 mg
Vitamin D	400 IU
Vitamin E	600 IU
Vitamin K (use natural sources such as alfalfa, green leafy vegetables)	100 mcg
Essential fatty acids (EFAs) (primrose oil, flaxseed oil, salmon oil, fish oil)	as directed on label

MINERALS	DAILY DOSAGES
Calcium	1,500 mg
Chromium (GTF)	150 mcg
Copper	3 mg

Iodine (kelp-good source)	225 mcg
Iron*	18 mg
Magnesium	750-1,000 mg
Manganese	10 mg
Molybdenum	30 mcg
Potassium	99 mg
Selenium	200 mcg
Zinc	50 mg

Iron should be taken only if a deficiency exists. Always take iron supplements separately, rather than in a multivitamin and mineral formula. Do not take iron with a supplement containing vitamin E.

(Reprinted by permission)

Now that's quite a list!!! If you ate a crummy diet, would you really need to take a pill for nearly every one of these nutrients? Doesn't it make sense that if our bodies really NEED all these nutrients, the most beneficial way to consume them would be in foods where they reside with all their best buddies?

Many micronutrients (phytochemicals) haven't even been named yet, but scientists know they exist. Separating nutrients from foods and making the choice of what's important and what's not, and processing those into a vitamin or mineral supplement seems to me like someone trying to play God with **my** health.

Start by eating colorful whole foods, as close to raw as possible. Take a high quality powdered juice product, with fiber and enzymes added. If you want to take a supplement, first give supplements like blackstrap molasses, brewer's yeast, and acidophilus a try. Eat several servings each day of dark green, leafy vegetables to supply essential minerals.

In our family, these simple methods have helped us feel better, look better, and succumb less often to common colds, flu, and other minor ailments (*and* to bounce back more quickly!).

Remember to start with **whole**some foods, and if possible, get help from a qualified nutritionist who believes in the nutritive value of foods. ❤

TABLES

What does it take to get a day's supply of calcium? (1000 mg.)

1 egg	28 mg	1 c. refried beans	141 mg
1 egg white	26 mg	1 c. soybeans	131 mg
1 apple	15 mg	1" slice tofu	108 mg
3 apricots	15 mg	1 oz. sunflower seeds	33 mg
1 avocado	19 mg	1 T. sesame seeds	11 mg
1 c. blackberries	36 mg	1 oz. English walnuts	27 mg
10 figs	269 mg	1 artichoke	47 mg
1/2 grapefruit	14 mg	1 c. asparagus	43 mg
1 c. grapefruit juice	22 mg	1 c. beet greens	164 mg
1 c. grape juice	23 mg	1 spear broccoli	205 mg
1 kiwifruit	20 mg	1 c. chinese cabbage	158 mg
1 orange	52 mg	1 c. carrots	48 mg
1 c. orange juice	27 mg	1 c. cauliflower	34 mg
1 pear	25 mg	1 c. celery	43 mg
1/4 c. raisins	28 mg	1 c. leaf lettuce	38 mg
1 c. raspberries	27 mg	1 c. chopped onions	40 mg
1 c. strawberries	21 mg	1 c. green peas	34 mg
1/2 slice watermellon	39 mg	1 c. sauerkraut	71 mg
1 bagel	29 mg	1 c. spinach (frozen)	277 mg
1 biscuit	47 mg	1 c. squash (summer)	49 mg
1 slice ww bread	32 mg	1 sweet potato	32 mg
1 pita	49 mg	1 c. mixed veggies (frozen)	46 mg
1 cup creamy wheat cereal	54 mg		
1 english muffin	96 mg		
1 oz. whole almonds	75 mg		
1 c. great northern beans	90 mg		
1 c. peas (navy)	95 mg		
1 c. pinto beans	86 mg		
1 c. garbanzo beans	80 mg		
1 c. lentils	50 mg		
1 oz. filberts	53 mg		
1 T. peanut butter	24 mg		

Calcium from these foods is more readily available to the body, so the amount of calcium required is much less than that needed if obtained from dairy products.

If you need a supplement, check out herbal calcium supplements that supply trace minerals to allow the body to make its own calcium. ♥

What does it take to get a day's supply of protein? (30g.)

(Research shows 30 grams to be completely adequate. The National Academy of Sciences' anti-cancer report warns against the consumption of too much meat and dairy products for protein. Eat plant foods instead!) All foods contain some protein. Protein-rich foods (from the plant kingdom) are most often found in vegetables, nuts, seeds, legumes, and grains. Eating a wide variety of foods, especially dark green, leafy vegetables, and including whole beans and grains will insure adequate protein intake. If in doubt, add a little protein powder to your smoothie!

1 egg	6 g	1 T. sesame butter	3 g
1 egg white	3 g	1 T. peanut butter	5 g
1 avocado	4g	1/4 c. pumpkin seeds	3 g
1 c. raisins	5g	1/4 c. sunflower seeds	8 g
1 bagel	7g	1 oz. pine nuts	3 g
1 c. barley	16g	1 oz. black walnuts	7 g
1 slice whole wheat bread	3 g	1 oz. almonds	6 g
1 pita	6 g	1 c. lentils, cooked	16 g
1 slice pumpernickel bread	3 g	1 c. split peas, cooked	16 g
1 c. Cream of Wheat	4 g	1 c. soybeans, cooked	20 g
1 c. rolled oats	6 g	1 c. asparagus	5 g
1 English muffin	5 g	1 c. corn, cooked	5 g
1 slice French toast	6 g	1 c. kale, cooked	4 g
1 c. macaroni or spaghetti	7 g	1 c. beet greens, cooked	4 g
1 c. egg noodles	7 g	1 c. spinach, cooked	5 g
1 sub sandwich roll	11 g	1 c. green peas, cooked	5 g
1 c. brown rice, cooked	5 g	1 potato, baked	5 g
1 c. whole wheat, cooked	5 g	1 c. sweet potatoes, cooked	5 g
1 c. Black beans, cooked	15 g	1 c. mixed veggies (frozen)	5 g
1 c. Lima beans, cooked	16 g		
1" piece tofu	9 g	*OR 3 T. rice or soy protein*	
1 oz. cashews	4 g	*powder!!* ❤	
1/4 c. sesame seeds	8 g		

What does it take to get a day's supply of carbohydrates (1200 calories from a 2000 calorie diet.)

It's easy to get too many calories if you're eating *simple* carbohydrates like refined white flours and sugars, soda pop, or even too many fruit juices. How? Carbohydrates are converted into energy by the body, and if you're eating too many *simple carbohydrates*, the body quickly converts them to energy and stores them as FAT! When you eat complex carbohydrates (WHOLE grains, WHOLE fruits, WHOLE veggies, WHOLE beans, and as close to raw as possible), it takes more time (and energy) for the body to digest them. They're more likely to be used for energy than stored as fat.

	Calories	Grams Carbohydrate
1 apple	80	21
1 c. applesauce, unsweetened	105	28
1 c. apple juice	115	29
3 apricots	50	12
1 avocado	340	27
1 c. banana, sliced	140	35
1 c. blueberries	80	20
10 cherries	50	11
10 dates	230	61
10 figs	475	122
1 grapefruit, peeled	150	39
1 c. grapefruit juice	95	23
10 grapes	35	9
1 c. grape juice	155	38
1 kiwi	45	11
1 mango	135	35
1 /2 cantaloupe	95	29
1/5 honeydew	90	24
1 nectarine	65	16
1 c. orange juice, fresh	110	26

	Calories	Grams Carbohydrate
1 c. papaya chunks	65	17
1 peach	35	10
1 pear	100	25
1 c. diced pineapple, raw	75	19
5 prunes	115	31
1/2 c. raisins	217	57
1 c. raspberries, raw	60	14
1 c. strawberries, raw	45	10
1 tangerine	35	9
1 c. diced watermelon	50	11
1 bagel	200	38
1 slice whole wheat bread	70	13
1 c. rolled oats, cooked	145	25
1 English muffin	140	26
1 slice French toast	155	17
1 c. egg noodles	200	37
1 c. macaroni or spaghetti noodles	190	39
1 c. brown rice	230	50
1 corn tortilla	65	13
1 c. brown rice, cooked	230	50
1 c. whole wheat, cooked	310	65
1 c. black beans, cooked	225	41
1 c. lima beans, cooked	260	49
1" piece tofu	85	3
1 oz. cashews	165	9
1/4 c. sesame seeds	180	3
1 T. sesame butter	90	3
1 T. peanut butter	95	42
1/4 c. pumpkin seeds	70	8
1/4 c. sunflower seeds	205	7
1 oz. almonds	165	6
1 c. lentils, cooked	215	38
1 c. split peas, cooked	230	42

	Calories	Grams Carbohydrate
1 c. soybeans, cooked	235	19
1 c. asparagus	45	8
1 carrot	30	7
1 c. corn, cooked	135	34
1 c. kale, cooked	40	7
1 c. beet greens, cooked	40	8
1 c. spinach, cooked	55	10
1 c. green peas, cooked	125	23
1 potato, baked	220	51
1 c. sweet potatoes, cooked	115	28
1 c. mixed veggies (frozen)	75	15
1 Jerusalem artichoke (sliced)	115	26
1 c. parsnips	125	30

When comparing the above "healthy choices" to refined carbohydrates, the numbers aren't much different, but remember that refined foods are processed much more quickly, and are much more likely to be stored as FAT.

ARTIFICIAL SWEETENERS
Don't be fooled into thinking artificial sweeteners aren't fattening. The body still reacts as if you've eaten sugar! You'd be much better off eating less of the real thing than loading up on harmful chemicals. ❤

Balch, James F. and Phyllis A. <u>Prescription for Nutritional Healing</u>. New York: Avery Publishing Group, 1997, pp. 3-62.

Hallberg, L. "Bioavailability of dietary iron in man," Annual Review of Nutrition 1:123-147, 1981.

Helman, A.D., and Darnton-Hill, I. "Vitamin and iron status in new vegetarians," American Journal of Clinical Nutrition 45:785-789, 1987.

Michael Colgan, Ph.D., CCN, <u>Optimum Sports Nutrition</u>. New York: Advanced Research Press, 1993

Townsley, Cheryl. <u>Food Smart</u>! Colorado: Pinion Press, 1994, pp. 97-124

Santillo, Humbart. <u>Food Enzymes, The Missing Link To Radiant Health</u>. Arizona: Hohm Press, 1993.

Bingham, Rita. <u>Food Combining, Better Health—The Natural Way</u>. Oklahoma: Natural Meals Publishing, 1998.

SEASONAL FOOD CHART FOR SMOOTHIES

April
bananas
pineapple
rhubarb
spinach
strawberries

May
bananas
celery
papaya
pineapple
strawberries
tomatoes
watercress

June
apricots
avocados
bananas
cantaloupe
cherries
figs
green peas
honeydew
limes
mangoes
nectarines
peaches
pineapple
plums

July
apricots
bananas
blueberries
cantaloupe
cherries
figs
nectarines
peaches
prunes
watermellon

August
apples
bananas
beets
berries
carrots
figs
melons
nectarines
peaches
pears
plums
tomatoes

September
apples
bananas
carrots
figs

September (cont'd)
grapes
greens
melons
pears
tomatoes

October
apples
bananas
grapes
persimmons

November
apples
bananas
cranberries
dates

December
apples
avocados
bananas
grapefruit
lemons
limes
oranges
pears
pineapple
tangerines
❤

PUBLICATIONS WORTH ORDERING

COUNTRY BEANS *by Rita Bingham*

Nearly 400 quick, easy meatless bean recipes with over 110 bean flour recipes, including FAST, fat-free 3-minute bean soups and 5-minute bean dips. Learn how to grind your own bean, pea and lentil flours, or where to purchase them.

Most recipes are wheat-free, gluten-free, and dairy-free. Recipes for every meal of the day. Guaranteed to change the way you use beans! **$14.95**

NATURAL MEALS IN MINUTES *by Rita Bingham*

Over 300 quick, high-fiber, low-fat, meatless recipes using wholesome storage foods. All meals made in 30 minutes or less!

- FAST meals using Grains and Beans
- Bean, Seed and Grain Sprouts
- 3-minute fat-free Powdered Milk Cheeses

Each recipe lists nutritional information. (Learn sneaky tricks for adding extra fiber to every meal.) Guaranteed to please! **$14.95**

THE NEW PASSPORT TO SURVIVAL *by Bingham/Dickey*

12 Steps To Self-Sufficient Living. How to survive natural, man-made, or personal disasters. Twelve easy steps to becoming self-sufficient, without panic! Includes quick mixes and heart-smart recipes to put you on the road to better health.

Learn what to store and why, where to store, and how to use what you store on a daily basis. **Learn what nutritious foods to store for only $150 per year per person! $15.95**

Quick **WHOLESOME FOODS** video with recipe booklet
by Bingham and Moulton

Whether you're preparing for emergencies, or just want to make quick, inexpensive meals, you'll learn to make easy recipes:

- Light, fluffy, 100% whole wheat breads
- Meatless spicy sausage, and thick steaklets
- Breakfasts, snacks and desserts using Whole Grains and Seeds
- Non-fat 3-minute powdered milk cheeses, including Country Chicken Fried Steak - mouthwatering and irresistible!
- 3-minute no-fat bean soups and cream sauces

Make delicious vegetarian meals in a FLASH. 65 minutes, VHS **$29.95**

1-2-3 SMOOTHIES *by Rita Bingham*

123 Quick Frosty Drinks - Delicious AND Nutritious! Is there one perfect breakfast—afternoon snack—meal-on-the-run—or one perfect way to sneak nutritious vitamins and other important nutrients into a finicky eater? YES! It's a 1-2-3 Smoothie! These energy-boosting, nutritious drinks are the hottest COOL healthy treats ever! 100% natural ingredients - no sugar, preservatives, artificial sweeteners, or added fat. **$14.95**

FOOD COMBINING Better Health—The *Natural* Way *by Rita Bingham*

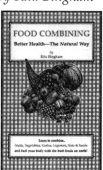

Take CHARGE of your health! Learn to use and combine the best foods on earth...*Fruits, Vegetables, Grains, Legumes, Nuts and Seeds.*

- Experience vibrant health
- Find and maintain your proper weight
- Learn how to prevent and even reverse illnesses such as cancer, heart disease, arthritis, and more!
- Complete protein meals—without animal products

80 pages. **$7.95**

OTHER VALUABLE PUBLICATIONS

Cookin' With Home Storage, by Tate and Layton. Over 700 recipes - Down home cookin' with the basics, Dutch oven cooking, sprouting, natural beauty & personal care. **$14.95** + $3.50 s&H. Call (435) 835-8283. *(Note: Some recipes contain processed oils and refined sugar.)*

Dynamic Health, and **An Apple A Day,** by Dr. M. Ted Morter. Call 1-800-281-4450 for more information on how to monitor your level of health by testing your body's reaction to acid foods.

Enzymes and Enzyme Therapy, by Dr. Anthony Cichoke. Keats Publishing, New Canaan, Connecticut.

Food Enzymes: The Missing Link to Radiant Health, by Humbart Santillo. Hohm Press, Prescott, AZ.

Feed Your Kids Right, and **Foods For Healthy Kids,** by Dr. Lendon Smith. Dell Publishing, New York, 10017. Illness, hyperactivity, and even stress can be prevented if your child eats right.

Food & Behavior, by Barbara Reed Stitt. Natural Press, P. O. Box 730, Manitowoc, WI 54221-0730. Learn the biochemical connection between the foods we eat, behavior and health.

The Amazing Wheat Book, by LeArta Moulton. This unique cook book can save you time and money. Find delicious, wholesome, fast recipes. Wheat meat, whole wheat breads, rolls, muffins, crackers, chips, soups, salads, and more. Prepare your own seasoning & sauce blends. Saves you money & eliminates preservatives. *(Note: Some recipes in this book contain refined sugar.)* **$14.95** + $3.50 s&H. Call (888) 554-3727.

The Food Storage Bible, by Jayne Benkendorf. A quick, easy reference guide for selecting thousands of healthful grocery products free of harmful preservatives. **$16.95** Call (800) 580-1414.

15 Minute Storage Meals, A Cookbook For the Busy Person, by Jayne Benkendorf. Learn the "Fabulous 30" high energy foods for better health, plus 30 tasty, low fat recipes for meals in only 15 minutes. Includes a one-month storage shopping list using items listed in The Food Storage Bible. **$12.95** Call (800) 580-1414.

EQUIPMENT AND SUPPLIES – SOURCES

BOB'S RED MILL, 5209 S. E. International Way, Milwaukie, OR 97222. (503) 654-3215. Freshly milled <u>bean</u>, <u>pea</u> and <u>lentil</u> <u>flours</u>, whole grains and whole grain products. The Mill also carries books and equipment. These products are available at many health stores across the U.S. Call or write Bob's for a supplier near you, or to ask for a catalog. If you're near the mill, visit the mill store.

BOSCH, Kitchen Specialties, distributes bread machines and flour mills. For information about Bosch Products available in your area, call (801) 263-8900. Kitchen Specialties is the exclusive distributor for Bosch Kitchen Products in the U. S. and Canada. They also carry the Zojirushi Home Bakery as well as the GrainMaster Whisper Mill, guaranteed to grind all beans and grains.

ECHO HILL COUNTRY STORE, RD1, Box 1029, Fleetwood, PA 19522. (610) 944-7358. Amish store supplying a wide variety of products, including bean, pea and lentil flours, bulk foods, cooking & baking supplies, books, quick mixes. Great mail-order or walk-in company.

EMERGENCY ESSENTIALS, 165 S. Mountain Way, Orem, UT 84058. 1-800-999-1863. 72-hour kits; camping, emergency and storage supplies, equipment, containers; MRE's, first aid kits, preparedness books and videos, foods, water purifiers, tents, backpack foods, supplies. Hand and electric grain mills. Great mail-order or walk-in company.

K-TEC, Orem, UT, manufacturer of Kitchen Mill and Champ Bread Mixer (with great heavy duty blender). 1-800-748-5400. Electric mill is guaranteed to grind all beans and grains. Autoknead feature on Champ Mixer turns mixer off when bread is ready for pans - usually only 3 to 5 minutes!

LIFE SPROUTS, 745 W. 8300 S., Paradise, UT 84328. 1-800-241-1516. An excellent source for sprouters, sprouting seeds and storage containers. Their seed mixes are specially combined to provide complete nutrition.

NATURAL MEALS PUBLISHING, 1-888-232-6706. **Preparedness books, cooking video, GSE** (an antimicrobial for first aid and water purification), and high-quality **juice powders with fiber and enzymes,** for storage and for better health.

WALTON FEED, INC, P. O. Box 307, Montpelier, ID 83254. 1-800-847-0465. Beans, grains, equipment, supplies, books, videos, storage containers, dehydrated foods, sprouting seeds, 72-hour kits. Hand-operated grain mills for cracking or grinding to a flour. Great source for co-op orders.

Alphabetical Index To Recipes

1-2-3 SMOOTHIES

Recipes by Category

1-2-3 SMOOTHIES